Jonathan Neal

REVERSE MO

What Every Financial Advisor Should Know

ISBN: 978-0-87218-980-5

Library of Congress Control Number: 2008944262

Copyright © 2009
The National Underwriter Company
P.O. Box 14367, Cincinnati, Ohio 45250-0367

Printed in U. S. A.

ABOUT THE AUTHOR

Jonathan Neal is a Senior Partner with CCG-Capital Consulting Group, LLC, and has twenty-nine years of experience in the retirement planning industry. He writes both consumer-oriented and industry-related articles on retirement planning topics and products that are frequently published in newspapers and financial magazines. He has also appeared on TV and radio programs across the country. As one of the original founders of the Society of Certified Long-Term-Care Advisors, he is recognized nationally as an authority on the issues within the field of long-term care, and he has clearly demonstrated his expertise in annuities by publishing numerous articles on the topic.

In addition to his articles, Mr. Neal has written over 20 Continuing Education Courses that have been approved by various state insurance departments on topics such as Professional Ethics, Long-Term Care, Retirement Planning, Fundamentals of IRAs, and the Concept of Stretching IRAs.

Mr. Neal has numerous industry-related designations and is a member of the following professional associations:

- IARFC: International Association of Registered Financial Consultants

- MDRT: Million Dollar Round Table

- NAFA: National Association for Fixed Annuities

- NAIFA: National Association of Insurance & Financial Advisors

- SCLTCA: Society of Certified Long-Term Care Advisors

- SCSA: Society of Certified Senior Advisors

Jonathan can be reached by email at www.jneal@ccgcap.com. (For additional information regarding speaking and/or training opportunities, please contract his speaking agent at www. Hohmangroup.Com.)

TABLE OF CONTENTS

Introduction...1

Section One: The Basics

Chapter 1: A Glimpse at an Emerging Market..............................9

Chapter 2: So What is a Reverse Mortgage?.............................15

    Accessing Funds Through a Reverse Mortgage........................18

    The Different Types of Reverse Mortgages.............................18

        Home Equity Conversion Mortgage (HECM)..................19

        Fannie Mae Home Keeper & Home Keeper for

        Home Purchase 20

        Jumbo Reverse Mortgages...21

    Deferred Payment Loans (DPLs) 21

    Property Tax Deferral (PTD)..22

    Contrasting Reverse Mortgages and Equity Loans....................22

Chapter 3: The Reverse Mortgage Product: A Brief History.......................23

Chapter 4: Things You Should Know Before a Client Asks 27

    Perception and Reality..29

Chapter 5: Why Use a Reverse Mortgage?.................................33

    Aggregate vs. Personal Inflation...34

    Dead Equity 35

Chapter 6: Is a Reverse Mortgage Right for Your Client?..........................39

Chapter 7: Reverse Mortgage Examples..................................47

    Mary Ann Finally Gets to Retire at 74 47

    David and Kathy Finally Go on that Cross Country Vacation....48

    Bill Remodels Their Home for Nancy 49

    Taking Care of Those Nagging Daily Expenses 49

    Reverse Mortgages and Long-Term Care................50

    Using Reverse Mortgages to Reduce Taxes............51

    Summary............................52

Chapter 8: What to Expect in an Actual Reverse Mortgage Proposal.........55

Section Two: Reverse Mortgages in the Financial Plan

Chapter 9: Reverse Mortgages, Taxes and Other Financial Products...........67

Chapter 10: Using Reverse Mortgage as a Tool to Reduce Income Tax.....75

Chapter 11: Value and Net Appreciation 87

    Asset and Liability....................................90

    Cost..92

    Value 95

Chapter 12: In Conclusion 97

    The Brave New World..............................99

Appendices

Appendix A: Federal Regulation Z..103

    Subpart E—Special Rules for Certain Home Mortgage

        Transactions 226.33 Requirements for
            Reverse Mortgages 103

    Appendix K to Part 226—Total Annual Loan Cost Rate
        Computations for Reverse Mortgage Transactions............105

Appendix B: HUD Handbook Appendix 22..115

Appendix C: HUD Field Offices..119

Glossary...125

Introduction

The purpose of this book is not to judge whether reverse mortgages are good or bad; it is not even about whether there should be regulation or supervision of these products. The primary reason for writing this book was to address the fact that reverse mortgages are here, and they are here to stay. As a financial or insurance advisor, refusing to accept this reality, or simply ignoring it, makes no sense. On the other hand, taking a position one way or the other without having a realistic understanding of what reverse mortgages are and how they can *(and should)* be used leaves one open to a charge of failing to keep up with the ever changing needs of seniors.

As the popularity of reverse mortgages grows, it is imperative that financial planners not only take the time to educate themselves on how these products work but also prepare themselves to play a significant role in their client's decision-making process when it comes to reverse mortgages.

Having said that, let me state, unequivocally, that I am not suggesting in any manner that producers should in any way look at reverse mortgages as a new product line or service; my position here is quite the contrary. I believe anyone working as a producer or planner in the financial industry should be extremely wary of receiving any type of compensation for the generation of a reverse mortgage, as this is venturing onto extremely thin ice from a conflict of interest viewpoint. Actually, let me rephrase that, I do not think any financial or insurance advisor should ever receive any type of remuneration from the generation of a reverse mortgage. And, as for the conflict of interest, any insurance or financial advisor that does benefit monetarily from the generation of a reverse mortgage is not on thin ice—they are in deep cold water.

What I do want to emphasize is that your expertise and professionalism can, and should, play a critical role in the planning process of any client who is considering a reverse mortgage; the implementation of a reverse mortgage will generate a new source of funds in the form of tax-free cash that will come in the form of a lump sum, a monthly payment, or as a line of credit. Regardless which of these three forms they choose to receive funds in, the end result will be a change in the make-up of their current financial plan.

A reverse mortgage is a stand-alone product, and, for the most part, there is little reason for you to be involved in this side of the process. On the other hand, in order to make the best possible use of this tax-free money, a complete review of the client's present financial position is something that you should address with your client, as there is nothing in the reverse mortgage process that gives adequate consideration on this subject. In addition, even though there is required financial consulting *(of sorts)* in the government-backed programs, the people responsible for doing that consulting do not present themselves as, nor should they be considered, financial planners.

After doing extensive research in the field of reverse mortgages, I have come to the conclusion that reverse mortgages are very viable products and should be given serious consideration by any senior looking for a way to unlock funds currently tied up in dead equity. Although rarely used in today's vernacular, I suspect that with the growing popularity of reverse mortgages, the term "dead equity" will become a commonly used phrase in the senior marketplace. In short, dead equity refers to those funds that are tied up in the equity buildup of the home in which a person lives. Although equity within one's house has always been accessible, its liquidity has always been tentative and restricted at best. For the most part, until the introduction of reverse mortgages, the equity buildup for most homeowners could only be accessed by the outright sale of the property or the creation of an equity loan that required both interest and principal repayment. In effect, dead equity is akin to having money on a deserted island—it is nice to have but it really is not doing anything for your client. Of course, we have all heard the old saying "you can't take it with you." Well, in the case of dead equity, your clients are not even using it while they are here.

The use of a reverse mortgage to unlock some of this dead equity provides the senior homeowner with the opportunity to generate a source of easily accessible, tax-free cash in a lump sum or on a recurring basis. This is where the expertise of the financial planner comes into play, as the proper use of these funds can dramatically change both the income and growth aspects of your client's portfolio. One such idea is the use of a monthly income stream generated from a reverse mortgage to replace income being generated from CDs or bonds. At present, the client has to pay income tax on this interest in addition to making it part of their Social Security and Medicare calculations. Of course, they could put this money into an annuity, but it really does not do anything for them as the interest they take for living expenses from the annuity is still taxable. However, by creating an income stream from a reverse mortgage, they can replace the taxable income with tax-free income. Now, if they put the original sum in a deferred annuity, they reduce their taxable income which, in turn, has a positive effect on their public benefit calculations. Another idea is to use the income from a reverse mortgage to pay premiums for long-term care and other types of insurance, which, in turn, will free up cash presently being used to keep any number of insurance policies in force. In many cases, the income generated from a reverse mortgage can provide the funds needed to allow seniors to purchase long-term care insurance that they otherwise would not be able to afford.

This is only the tip of the iceberg. There are as many different reasons for a senior to use a reverse mortgage as there are people taking them out. Even though some of those reasons, like the remodeling of a home, using the funds to take a vacation, or purchasing a motor home or vacation home may not necessarily have an effect on their financial well being, the use of a reverse mortgage to purchase long-term care insurance, or for that matter any other type of insurance, does have an effect. In reality, it really doesn't matter why a client looks into a reverse mortgage. What does matter is that as their financial advisor, you have an obligation to help them make the best use of the funds they will be receiving in conjunction with those funds you already have under management.

In all likelihood, the popularity of reverse mortgages is going to continue to grow. And, as it does, it is going to change how seniors look at their overall portfolios. Unfortunately, there are also going to be more and more seniors who do not take into consideration the effect a reverse mortgage will have on their portfolio and estate. So remember, even though we will not share in the fees generated from the implementation of reverse mortgages, we cannot ignore our responsibly as professionals to serve our clients' best interests.

It does not really matter how we as insurance planners, financial planners, and advisors feel about reverse mortgages. Like them or not, there are a lot more reasons to believe that reverse mortgages will continue to grow in popularity than there are that their popularity will decrease.

The above comment is not based on my *(or for that matter anyone else's)* opinion. It is based on the following facts…

- In order to qualify for a reverse mortgage, the home owner or owners have to be at least 62 years old and have equity in their home. Now, combine that with these two words—"baby boomers." This represents a huge market that will continue to grow for the next 20 years or more.

- Boomers are those 78 million Americans born between 1946 and 1964 who now make up somewhere around 26% of our population, compared to the 41 million Gen-Xers born between 1968 and 1976 who make up about 13.5% of our population. The importance in comparing the baby boomers with the Gen-Xers is best illustrated by Social Security Administration projections: In 2031, when there will be 57.8 million baby boomers still with us between the ages of 66 and 84, there will only be 2.1 workers for each Social Security beneficiary, as compared to today where we have 3.3 workers for each Social Security beneficiary.

- Based on numerous surveys that have been conducted, only 34% of boomers think they will have enough money to live comfortably after they retire. Forty percent are not sure whether or not they will have enough money to live comfortably and the remaining 29% are seriously concerned about having enough money to live on, let alone to live comfortably. Aside from those statistics, it appears that one-fourth of Boomers do not think they will have enough money to retire and will continue to work indefinitely.

- The ever increasing cost of health care for seniors is a serious issue. According to the Bureau of Labor Statistics, "when budgeting medical expenses, baby boomers should expect increased health-care spending as they age." For instance, in 2004 those aged 55 to 64 spent $3,262 and those 65 and over, $3,899 on health care. When adjusted for inflation in the health care industry, we can adjust those numbers to $4,163 for those aged 55 to 64 and for those 65 and over $4,976 (*or 19.5% more for the same standard of health care*).

Now think about the following for a minute...

- There are more Americans over 62 years old today then there were yesterday, and there are going to be more people over 62 years old tomorrow than there are today. And that is going to be true for many years to come.

- Due to the growth in the number of those receiving Social Security benefits and the decline in the number of people paying into the Social Security system, the federal government will not be able to increase benefits for retirees in the future and, in all likelihood, will have to decrease benefits.

- As the number of people over 65 continues to increase, the cost of health care for that group will also continue to increase.

- For average Americans over 65 years old, their home represents 49.6% of their total net worth and it is not producing any income.

Although opinions may differ as to their need or the advantage of using a reverse mortgage, it is very hard to deny that the evidence is overwhelming, and the use of this product will continue to grow. This leaves only one question for planners and advisors to address. Are they going to learn what they need to know about reverse mortgages in order to provide their clients with advice about how using a reverse mortgage will affect their portfolio? Or are they going to ignore this area all together and offer no opinion about reverse mortgages to their clients at all?

Section One
The Basics

A Glimpse at an Emerging Market

By the time most Americans reach 62, they are retired or in the later stages of planning to retire. What many newly retired people have to come to grips with is the often stark reality that their primary source of income (earnings produced through work) stops. More often than not, this results in life style changes few are prepared for.

Social Security, retirement plans, and personal assets will now be the main sources of income for retirees. According to a 2005 report published by the U.S. Department of Health and Human Services and the U.S Department of Commerce, money received from Social Security makes up 39% of income for people 65 and older. The following chart illustrates the sources of income for people over 65.

Figure 1.1

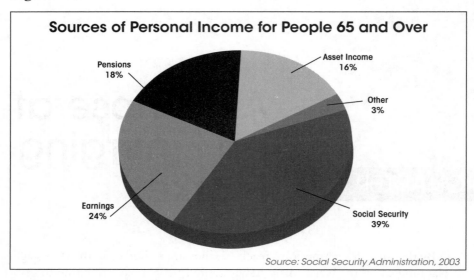

Sources of Personal Income for People 65 and Over

Pensions
18%

Asset Income
16%

Other
3%

Earnings
24%

Social Security
39%

Source: Social Security Administration, 2003

Most people understand that the amount of income they will have available after they retire will be less, and in some cases dramatically less, than they enjoyed prior to retirement, but few are truly prepared for this actuality.

The failure to fully take into consideration the realities of post-retirement income needs by the average person and far too many so-called "retirement planners" is a problem that only gets bigger the longer a retiree lives. A 2004 U.S. Census Bureau report brought this point home when it compared the median household incomes for seniors. The following chart illustrates how the median income decreases with age.

Figure 1.2

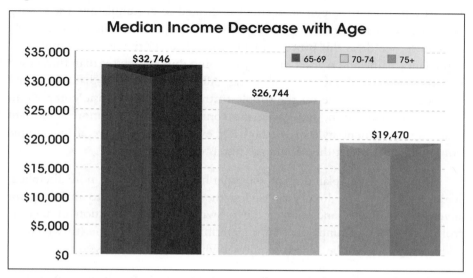

I think we would be safe in assuming that the average 65 year old does not make plans based on having his income drop by some 18% by the time he reaches 70, let alone be prepared to have another decline of 27% by the time he reaches 75. Yet, according to the U.S. Census Bureau data, the median household income for American retirees will drop 40.5% in as little as ten years.

The problem here is three-fold. First, many Americans do little to no retirement planning. Second, those that do often fail to take into consideration the effect that taking distributions from their assets (regardless of whether such distributions are in accordance with their income needs) has on their nest eggs. Third, and by far, the biggest challenge for people in our profession is that far too many "retirement planners" have put too *much* emphasis on the accumulation phase and too *little* on the distribution phase when it comes to retirement plans, models, and forecasts.

Why does it seem like there are so many retirement planners and so few post-retirement planners?

In fact, there are any number of reasons. None, however, more obvious than that it is so much easier to accumulate funds over a long period of time than it is to manage those funds in such a way as to ensure clients will always have the money that they will need to maintain an acceptable life style.

Think about it. The basic retirement planning model is not only simple, it is easy to operate. Open an account dedicated to accumulating assets, keep putting money into it over a long period of time, and let the market work. Of course, we dress this process up and call whatever method we employ by some fancy name and market our way of doing things as better than those used by other planners doing the same thing. All the time hoping that clients and prospects never stumble on the simple truth that the three basic components of time, diversification, and systematic contributions are far more important than any investment style or method. Or even worse, that we all use simple computer models that they could use just as easily.

Post-retirement planning, on the other hand, requires a lot more discipline; it does not have the luxury of having the market or time to make up for investment mistakes and market down swings. The distribution of income from a set block of funds over an undetermined period of time (to which no additional funds will be added) requires a whole different skill set.

The truth is that counting on the positive long-term effects of the equity markets is not always the correct answer in every situation. One such occurrence is when needs shift from accumulation to distribution. Counting on clients' assets to produce the income they need to live on is a totally different ballgame than just letting the assets sit and accumulate over a long period of time.

When it comes to generating income for retirees, many financial planners only take the following sources into consideration: Social Security and other government-based retirement programs, pensions and other retirement plans such as 401(k)s and IRAs, and interest/dividends from individual savings and investments.

The misconception is that retirement income is based on a three-legged stool: Social Security, pension plans (private and/or corporate) and personal savings. Unfortunately this concept fails to take into consideration the obvious: for approximately 50% of all retirees—their home represents the single largest asset they own. It is hard to understand why so many "retirement planning professionals" do not take into consideration such a readily accessible source of income from an asset that represents such a large percentage of their portfolio.

The following chart shows just how dominant the value of a home is in the total protfolio of Americans over 65.

Figure 1.3

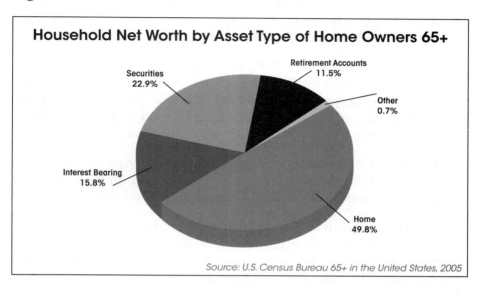

Household Net Worth by Asset Type of Home Owners 65+

Retirement Accounts
11.5%

Securities
22.9%

Other
0.7%

Interest Bearing
15.8%

Home
49.8%

Source: U.S. Census Bureau 65+ in the United States, 2005

It only takes a glance at the above chart to realize that for most seniors the money they have tied up in their homes is, in fact, their primary source of wealth. Although I have not found any survey or study that has published results on this issue, the numerous interviews and conversations I have had with both retirees and planners leads to this conclusion. It appears (at least to me) that the reason most financial planners do not take the home into consideration is that it is outside their normal business models. Retirees, on the other hand, by and large seem to be under the impression that in order to access the cash tied up in home equity they only have three options available. All of which they tend to find less than attractive.

They could sell their present home, then purchase another home, or pay rent for the rest of their lives. They could take out a new mortgage; however, this would introduce a new payment in the form of a mortgage. They could take out an equity line of credit, but, this again results in repayment. In addition, many home loan groups are not interested in writing mortgages and equity loans for retired people without work-related income.

The failure by both retirees and planners to take into consideration the opportunities a reverse mortgage can provide can only be explained as the result of either a lack of understanding of how the product works, or that they do not even know it exists. What is so unfortunate is that they fail to even consider that the equity buildup in the homes of people 62 and older can add a fourth leg to the heretofore three-legged retirement income stool.

The key to adding this fourth leg is to take advantage of the opportunities a reverse mortgage can provide a home owner, by way of accessing a portion of their equity without the need to find a new place to live or generate and pay new payment obligations. For many retirees, a reverse mortgage may be able to present additional interesting options such as tax reduction.

In some cases, a reverse mortgage can provide retirees with an option that will have a dramatic effect on their standard of living. In others, a reverse mortgage can be used to make positive changes in their tax status.

The key for these retirees is to get the right information they need to truly consider how a reverse mortgage might affect their retirement. The best way for them to achieve that goal is by consulting with a trusted financial advisor who understands the "ins and outs" of reverse mortgages as well as what impact the (tax-unencumbered) cash their clients can expect from a reverse mortgage will have on their retirement plans.

This leaves financial planners with both an obligation and an opportunity. The obligation is to better serve an ever-growing senior population by learning how reverses mortgages work. The opportunity is to demonstrate professionalism through education in an effort to stay abreast with the ever-changing needs of the world American seniors live in.

So What is a Reverse Mortgage?

CHAPTER 2

According to the National Reverse Mortgage Lending Association (NRMLA) at www.nrmla.com, a reverse mortgage is *"a unique loan that enables homeowners 62 and over to convert a portion of the equity in their homes into tax-free income without having to sell the home, give up title, or take on a new monthly mortgage payment."*

That is straight forward and simple enough. Unfortunately, there is so much misinformation being circulated within the market place that, in order to understand and explain this product, we must take a much more in-depth look into not only what it is but also what it is not.

The first thing we need to do is address the differences between reverse and traditional mortgages. The most apparent difference is that the lender holds title on the home and the borrower makes payments with a traditional mortgage. In a reverse mortgage, the borrower holds title and the lender makes payments.

The reverse mortgage is a special type of home loan that lets homeowners convert a portion of the equity in their principal residence into cash. Unlike a traditional mortgage, home equity loan, or second mortgage, however, no repayment is required until the homeowner no longer lives in the home. Another important difference is that unlike a traditional mortgage, second mortgage, or home equity line of credit (where the homeowner must first qualify financially and is then required to make regular payments) a reverse mortgage provides the homeowner with access to a portion of the equity without having to qualify for the loan or incurring any payments.

Another way to look at the differences between traditional and reverse mortgages is by looking at the debt/equity ratio. In a traditional mortgage, monthly payments reduce the debt and increase the ownership or what is referred to as "equity." As these loans are amortized in the earlier years, the majority of the homeowner's payments go to interest, while very little is applied to the principal (equity). As the mortgage matures and less of the payment is required for interest, more goes towards equity. The result is that as the amount of money borrowed is reduced so is the interest portion of each payment. In fact, as the debt is reduced, the homeowner's equity position increases until the mortgage is paid off, resulting in the amount of equity and the value of the home being equal.

In a traditional mortgage, as the amount of principal owed is reduced, the homeowner's equity increases. One should remember that the amount of each required payment does not change. What changes over time is the amount of each payment that is dedicated to interest and principal. The following graph demonstrates how an amortization schedule works.

Figure 2.1

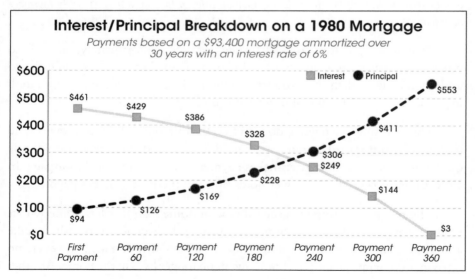

The opposite is true with a reverse mortgage: the homeowner is taking money out rather than paying money in. As the homeowner withdraws money from a reverse mortgage, his equity position is reduced. The homeowner is in fact creating a debt position that is not required to be paid off until the homeowner leaves the residence permanently or passes away. It is important to understand that by implementing a reverse mortgage, the homeowner is, in essence, borrowing money from himself. Over the life of the mortgage, the interest accumulates not only on the principal amount withdrawn from the equity, but also on the ever-growing amount of interest. Thus, as the principal and interest accumulate, the homeowner's equity is reduced.

Another thing we need to take into consideration is just what makes up the equity in a home. I think a lot of people would think differently about reverse mortgages if they took a moment to consider the three different types of money that make up equity.

The first is the original amount of the mortgage (which we refer to as the "principal"). The second is the amount of interest paid on that principal over the years that the loan is active. The third is the growth in the value of the property over any period (which is reflected by the market value). When we take all three of these components together, we can calculate what I like to refer to as the "net appreciation." The following graph illustrates the changes that occur over time in the three different parts of home equity.

Figure 2.2

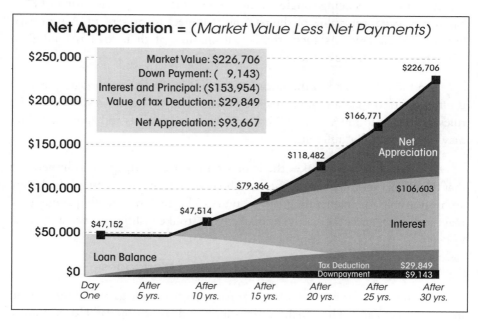

- 17 -

Accessing Funds Through a Reverse Mortgage

Reverse mortgages generally offer three different ways for homeowners to access their money: on a monthly basis, in the form of a line of credit, or as a lump sum. The amount of money they have access to by way of a reverse mortgage is limited.

The actual amount of loan homeowners can qualify for is based on four separate contingencies:

(1) The age of the homeowner (or if the property is held in joint name, the youngest owner must be at least 62 years old).

(2) The amount of equity in the home; generally homeowners must have an equity position of no less than 35%.

(3) The current interest rate being offered by the mortgage company chosen.

(4) The appraised value of their home.

However, there is a caveat to number four because it depends on what type of reverse mortgage is being sought. If the homeowners are applying for an FHA-based mortgage, the value of their home is subject to present FHA mortgage limits for their area. As such, the actual amount of their loan is limited to whichever is the lesser of those two.

On the other hand, if the homeowners are applying for a private (or what is often referred to as a jumbo) reverse mortgage, they are not restricted by the rules that apply to FHA loans. Consequently, loan amounts and appraisal values may be dramatically different.

Regardless of who makes the loan for a reverse mortgage, it is imperative that the clients are fully aware that after the reverse mortgage is established, they are responsible for maintaining the property. This includes timely payments of real estate taxes and other conventional payments like utilities, as well as general upkeep.

The Different Types of Reverse Mortgages

At this time, there are three primary reverse mortgages being offered in the marketplace. They include the oldest and most popular Home Equity Conversion Mortgage (HECM), the Fannie Mae Home Keeper & Home

Keeper for Home Purchase, and the Jumbo Reverse Mortgage (introduced to address the needs of people whose home values are higher than the FHA and Fannie Mae lending limits).

Home Equity Conversion Mortgage (HECM)

First introduced in 1989, this reverse mortgage program is backed by the United States Department of Housing and Urban Development through the Federal Housing Administration. Representing well over 85% of all reverse mortgages, this program is far and away the most commonly used reverse mortgage today.

Like all reverse mortgages, qualifying for this program revolves around three primary components: (1) the age of the borrower, (2) the initial interest rate, which changes to reflect current rates, and (3) the value of the borrower's home. On the surface, these three appear to be simple enough to understand and, in reality, the first two are. However, the method used to actually determine the amount of the third component, the "value of the home," lends itself to confusion. Prior to October 2008, a fourth component was added that was not found in other reverse mortgage products. This component took into consideration the actual location of the home: the maximum amount a borrower was eligible to receive was limited by the HECM maximum lending limits that in many cases did not come close to reflecting the true value of the home. It is important to remember that these limits had been established by the FHA and did not take into consideration many factors that can reflect the realities of free marketplace. One of the biggest misgivings of the calculations used to establish these loan limitations was that they were arrived at on a county by county basis. This flew in the face of the oldest and most fundamental bywords in the real estate industry— "location, location, location." Owing to this, there were often significant differences between the lending limits and the actual values of comparative homes and their true market values within a relatively small statistical or geographic area. At that time, the lending limits for this program ranged between $200,160 and $362,790.

Whether intended or not, when the overall market place was taken into consideration, those county-by-county limits could end up generating statistical anomalies. An example of this would be two homeowners that lived within the same county. One home was appraised at $200,000 and the other at $400,000. Even though the second had a market value of twice that of the first, the first would qualify for a loan that represented a significantly higher percentage of the home's value.

As of October 2008, a single national limit of $417,000 applied. But, for reverse mortgage credit approvals issued during 2009, the American Recovery and Reinvestment Act of 2009 allows a maximum dollar increase of 50%—currently $625,500 based on the $417,000 limit).

Another aspect of the Home Equity Conversion Mortgage (HECM) program that ends up being a double-edged sword is the fees associated with creating the reverse mortgage. On one hand, the United States Department of Housing and Urban Development (HUD) can protect borrowers from being overcharged on certain fees, such as the initial deposit a borrower can be charged to put the required Mortgage Insurance Protection (MPI, also known as IMPI) in place as well as the maximum premium that can be charged on an annual basis to keep this insurance protection in effect. There is also a maximum amount a lender can earn on a mortgage. On the other hand, these same controls significantly reduce competition that (generally) is not to the advantage of the marketplace. In addition to those fees and charges that have maximum limits set on them by the FHA, the borrower is also responsible for standard closing costs associated with the mortgage such as title insurance, registration, taxes, and attorney fees. These are not set and, as such, are subject to negotiation.

Fannie Mae Home Keeper & Home Keeper for Home Purchase

A few years after HUD introduced its reverse mortgage program, Fannie Mae saw a need for those owners whose situations were not covered by the HECM and introduced its own reverse mortgage program that they named "Home Keeper®." Although similar in many ways to the HECM program, the differences are significant. The most noticeable is the maximum mortgage limit, which (at the time of the writing of this book) is $417,000 in the Fannie Mae program. This is $54,210 (or 14.9%) higher than the limits of the HECM program. The Fannie Mae program is also much more "user friendly" to people looking to access debt equity in condominiums and multiple-unit dwellings.

One of the more interesting ways to use a reverse mortgage is to utilize the proceeds that can be generated from a reverse mortgage on a home presently being lived in to purchase a new home. In other words, if a person had a home from which she could generate enough cash, she could write a reverse mortgage on that home and use the lump sum payment to purchase a new home (which in effect allows the borrower to complete a transaction on the new home on a cash basis). The advantage of such a transaction is that it puts any equity remaining from the old home (after it is sold and the reverse mortgage is paid off) into the homeowner's pocket. In addition, the new home (which has already been paid for) automatically becomes eligible for a new reverse mortgage.

Jumbo Reverse Mortgages

Also known as "Conventional" or "Private Reverse Mortgages," these reverse mortgages are offered by private companies and are *not* insured by the federal government in any manner. They are not required to follow any of the guidelines set forth by the FHA. However, (in many cases) they do include such things as the mandatory counseling and the nonrecourse features that can limit the amount the homeowner can borrow even though the lender can make a loan based on a greater percentage of the property's market value.

These mortgages are generally more attractive to owners of higher-valued homes as the loans are based on the actual appraisal value rather than being subject to FHA limits. Another thought to consider with these reverse mortgages is that the upfront cost is often less than that found in the FHA or HECM programs. The interest rates charged on these loans are typically tied to a pre-determined index and (in many cases) are adjustable. As such, it is important for borrowers to make sure that they are fully aware of how much interest is being charged and what, if any, limits are applicable regarding future interest rates.

Even for people who do not have higher-valued homes, it is often advantageous to compare the FHA and HECM reverse mortgages with these conventional programs. In many instances, borrowers will find that the lenders from whom they are getting quotes for their reverse mortgage also offer one or more of these conventional programs.

Deferred Payment Loans (DPLs)

This is a program offered by some municipal, county, and state government agencies. DPLs are a type of reverse mortgage that offer a one-time, lump sum payment based on the equity borrowers have in their homes. They require no prepayment of the initial loan or any interest, until the owner no longer lives in that home. Generally these programs are put in place as an effort by the local government to rebuild and improve neighborhoods within a specific area. As an extra incentive to those homeowners willing to play their part in the revitalization of neighborhoods, some local governments are willing to forgive part or all of these loans if the borrower stays in that home for a certain length of time.

In most cases, these types of reverse mortgages are limited in their scope. Unlike the federal programs, age is often not an issue, but the income of the borrower and the value of a property often does make a significant difference. In most cases, the government agency backing these programs requires that the borrower use the funds for repairs or improvement only.

Property Tax Deferral (PTD)

Limited in scope and depending on where a person lives, there are some county and state government agencies that allow property owners to use this type of reverse mortgage. The sole purpose of this program is to provide the homeowner with a loan based on equity to pay their property tax. The amounts of these loans are generally limited by the amount of property tax due in a specific year. In most cases, the amount that can be borrowed over the lifetime of this type of loan is limited. In addition, PTD loans are not permitted to be subordinate to other loans. As such, a person who is using one of these (and has an outstanding balance) would not be eligible for any other type of reverse mortgage.

Contrasting Reverse Mortgages and Equity Loans

The primary difference between reverse mortgages and equity loans is found in the form of repayment of the loan or mortgage. In both cases, the equity homeowners have built up in their home is being used as collateral. With an equity loan, repayment of principal and interest begins immediately. This, in turn, requires borrowers to deduct from their income the amount required to meet monthly payments or to generate income from some other source to maintain the loan. With a reverse mortgage, borrowers are not required to make any payments. Further, their income is increased by the money they receive from the reverse mortgage.

Another way to look at it is an equity loan requires regular payments throughout the duration of the loan; whereas, a reverse mortgage has no required payments during the life of the loan and is settled in full at the conclusion.

The Reverse Mortgage Product: A Brief History

CHAPTER 3

Reverse mortgages have been around for a long time. In fact, they have been around long enough that many companies are now distributing marketing material in which words such as "New Generation" and "New Look" are part of their marketing phrases in an attempt to separate their products from earlier versions of reverse mortgages.

It could be argued that those "first-generation" reverse mortgages left the marketplace with a negative impression. I am not sure that would be an accurate or fair statement as I believe the product has always offered value; however, it would be hard to deny that the original marketing (in particular the people who were doing the one-on-one presentations to prospects) may have been the cause of the slow start for this product.

I remember when I was first introduced to reverse mortgages. I was working on a project with a gentleman by the name of Mike Bowers who was, and still is, one of the most impressive people I have ever met in the financial/insurance field. As a matter of fact, if someone asked me to describe the prefect president of a company, I would describe Mike. At that time he was the president of a large broker dealer and we were working together on a project that involved introducing a product designed to meet the specific needs of seniors to high-end financial planners. It was during this time while we worked together that Mike invited me to attend one of his company's producers' conventions. At this conference, Mike introduced me to a young lady by the name of Melissa Nelson, who at that time was marketing reverse mortgages. Melissa was extremely professional and it was obvious that she knew the reverse mortgage business inside out. I knew Mike would not expose his company or producers to any product of a company that was not top shelf, and I felt confident of Melissa's credibility. Because of these two people and my belief that the product had great value, my initial introduction to reverse mortgages was very positive. I was so impressed that I invited Melissa to speak about reverse mortgages at a number of senior-focused training courses that my company was conducting.

Unfortunately all of my good feelings were shaken by the actions of one person. Usually, once a year I gathered all the larger producers I work with in a geographical area together for a work shop so we can share and discuss ideas. I was holding one of these in Savannah and invited Melissa. She accepted the invitation and asked if she could bring along a local mortgage broker to which I agreed. In any event, I let this man speak to our group and (after less than five minutes) I realized this was a mistake. Rather than cover reverse mortgages, he went into some type of old-fashioned hard sales story that was totally inappropriate for the occasion. Besides missing the point he was supposed to be covering, he was trying to impress a group of highly professional sales people with his hard sale stories. Finally, when it became apparent that his presentation was geared to ending up with the client's money is *his* pocket, I cut him off.

What I took away from this was that the problem the reverse mortgage industry was facing was mainly due to the street level contact people. I knew that Mike, Melissa, and I felt good about this product and the needs it could meet in the market place. In short, it seemed like a good product being introduced at the right time to the right market. Unfortunately, for whatever reason, by and large the initial sales force proved to be a weak link. As a result, the public was dealing with a sales force that was not representing the product (or the companies) in a professional manner.

This has been true with a number of new products when they first entered the market. In the case of reverse mortgages, I believe that this contributed greatly to its slow start. This story does have a happy ending. The reverse mortgage brokers that I run into today are much more professional and better trained. This, of course, is an example of a maturing market that is a reflection of information dissemination through better trained and more professional sales people.

Regardless of how reverse mortgages were marketed and who was selling them, it is clear to see by the dramatic increase in sales over the past few years that the reverse mortgage products being offered today are far superior to the original products. It is also apparent that the people selling reverse mortgages today are better trained and more aware of their customers' needs than their predecessors were. The following graph illustrates the growth of reverse mortgages in the U.S from 1990-2008.

Figure 3.1

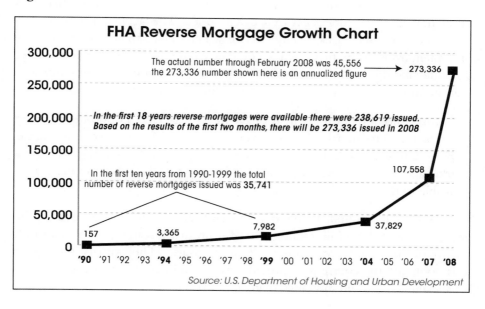

It should, however, not be misconstrued that the original versions of reverse mortgages were all bad. In reality, reverse mortgages have always been viable products when used in appropriate situations. Most of the negative impressions left by the original products are rooted in the sad but unavoidable fact that some clients obtained reverse mortgages when they were not the best vehicles to meet their needs and desires. It is not my intent to dwell on where these negative perceptions originated, nor is it my intent to promote the latest versions of reverse mortgages as end-alls to the various income problems a senior may face.

In my personal opinion, reverse mortgages are neither good nor bad, but rather simply a tool that is available to homeowners over 62 years of age. Like any financial product, when used in the correct situation, they can be very advantageous. On the other hand, when employed improperly, they tend to end up being mistakes. There is only one reason a product that has been on the market as long as reverse mortgages have can still be so misunderstood: poor marketing.

Yet, this does not minimize the fact that (rightly or wrongly) the general reaction to reverse mortgages is one of negativity and suspicion. This point was driven home to me time and again while writing this book. It did not matter whether the person was 75 or 35; whenever I told someone I was writing a book about reverse mortgages, more often than not, they told me that they thought that reverse mortgages were bad products. The fact that in almost every case they were totally lacking any facts on which to base their opinions did not stop them from stating them with vigor. The truth is that when I was first asked to undertake this book, I also had a negative impression oft reverse mortgages, but the more research I did, the more my opinion changed.

I have no dog in this fight, as I have never marketed, nor do I ever expect to market, reverse mortgages. However, as the popularity of reverse mortgages continues to grow, I feel it is imperative for any person working in the senior market and dealing with other people's money to understand all the alternatives available to them.

With that in mind, I have done a significant amount of research on this topic and used the information gathered from that research to write not only this book, but also a continuing education course. The primary purpose of this book and the course is to provide insight and education to people in the financial planning and insurance fields about reverse mortgages.

You may or may not like the reverse mortgage concept, but only a fool would fail to see that reverse mortgages are playing an ever-increasing part in post-retirement income planning. Combine this reality with the demographic realities seniors play in the United States, and you are forced to face the reality that those working in the senior market place have to choose between one of two alternatives: either learn this product and how it can be used by your retired cliental or be left behind. More and more retirees are going to see the advantageous options reverse mortgages can provide them and they are going to take advantage of those options, either with or without you playing a part in the decisions.

Things You Should Know Before a Client Asks

CHAPTER 4

There are four basic issues you should take into consideration before making any recommendation to your clients prior to them making a decision to implement a reverse mortgage.

The first thing you should suggest they consider is whether they should do an FHA-backed reverse mortgage or a private reverse mortgage. Although there are numerous differences between the two, the primary difference is the amount that can be borrowed against the market value of a home. In addition, other areas that need to be considered are interest rates, loan generation costs, and maintenance fees, all of which should be shopped and compared before deciding which of these two methods best suit your client's needs.

The second thing you need to spend time thinking about is exactly what it is your client intends to do with the money. As to whether or not you think the money is being put to good use is not important. What is important is that you take the time to listen to how your client wants to use the money. Most people do not even consider a reverse mortgage until an actual need arises. In many cases, clients start coming up with all kinds of ideas that have nothing to do with their original needs after they get an idea as to how much money they might be able to receive. There is nothing wrong with this; however, like most things in life, prior consideration is almost always better then reflection. The primary idea you want to convey is that advance planning generally gives more and better options and removes the time limitations that more often than not restrict choices.

More and more often I see clients setting up reverse mortgages even though they have no pressing needs for any money. The reason for this appears to be that they want ready access to cash in case an opportunity presents itself. Some might feel that the initial cost associated with putting a reverse mortgage in place for some possible future use is an expensive proposition. However, arguments can be made that having ready access to a large sum of money in the event of a future need or opportunity is worth the cost.

In any case, you cannot be too far off base by recommending that your clients should have a fairly good idea as to what it is they intend to do with the money they receive from a reverse mortgage.

The third thing that should be considered, and is by far most often over looked, is how this influx of cash will affect the rest of your client's portfolio. For whatever reason, most people do not consider the effect that an inflow of tax-free cash from the reverse mortgage can have on their lifestyle.

If clients are taking a monthly distribution to pay typical bills such as prescription drugs, insurance premiums, utilities, etc., there will be an immediate effect on their monthly budget. The result of this new source of income being received will be the freeing up of money from their original budget that was dedicated to those bills. This will leave them with the question of what to do with the money here-to-for being spent on those bills, prescriptions, etc.

If the funds from a reverse mortgage are used to pay off debt such as a credit card or car loan, this again frees up money from their original budget; once again the need to take into consideration how that freed-up money will be put to use and that is something better considered prior to, rather than after, the fact.

If, on the other hand, they borrow a lump sum to remodel their home, put on an addition, or something of that nature, they would be well served to take into consideration the cost of maintenance and upkeep and how these will factor in their monthly budget. I know of one couple who added an enormous closed-in porch that they had always wanted. They loved that porch and used it extensively; the only problem came after they used all the money they could get from the reverse mortgage to build and furnish it. It only took a couple of years before they learned the hard way that their failure to take into consideration the additional cost required for heating and cooling such a large space. Now they do not use it as much as they would like because their monthly budget cannot meet the cost of the additional power required to keep the room open year round.

The final issue that you need being to your clients' attention is the form in which they intend to receive the money. As mentioned previously, this can either be taken on a monthly income basis, in a lump sum, or in the form of a line of credit.

My recommendation would almost always be that they establish the loan at the highest possible amount, regardless of the sum they initially intend to spend. It is also my opinion that they do this in the form of a line of credit.

The reasoning behind this is that a line of credit provides more flexibility than the lump sum or the monthly income option. Keep in mind that with a line of credit option, the client is not incurring interest on the money until it is withdrawn. This, in effect, provides for the most cost-efficient and also the largest amount of money that can be accessed if and when the need or a desire arises.

Perception and Reality

A couple of years ago, my mother fell ill and I ended up spending a week in my home town. I grew up in a steel mill town in Western Pennsylvania and moved right after graduation. I had rarely been back for more than a day or two at a time since. My mother was in the hospital and, even though I spent hours with her every day, I still had a lot of time on my hands. As a result, I had an opportunity to visit with some old high school friends. One evening, a few of us got together for dinner. One of the topics of conversation during dinner was that I was the only one in the group who went to college rather than the mill! There were a number of reasons for this, not the least being that when we were in high school, the steel mills of Western PA appeared to offer an extremely good alternative to college. The pay was very good, the benefits were excellent, and none of us ever thought that the day would come that the mills would close down. Unfortunately, not only for my friends but for thousands of families in that area, they did close down, and my friends who spent their twenties and early thirties in those good union jobs have since found those high-paying hourly jobs and those union-won benefit packages hard to replace. In any event, after listening to two of my friends relate stories about how they were struggling, I responded by saying that I also struggled. At this point, my best friend turned to me and said, "Yeah, that may be, but then you struggle on a whole different level." That comment drove a point home to me. Something I knew but never saw from a personal point of view. The fact is that income and financial struggles are not mutually exclusive, the only difference is the level on which one struggles.

The opportunities to generate new or higher income from work make the relationship between incomes and struggles even more profound for retired people. Therefore, the understanding of where and how their income is generated is of great importance to the elderly.

The extent to which an individual retiree is dependent on Social Security varies greatly. The amount of Social Security (or other government-related retirement plan) a person receives is of little relevance, whereas the percentage of their income that depends on those government dollars is of great importance.

Figure 4.1 shows the percentage of income that Social Security represents for different groups.

Figure 4.1

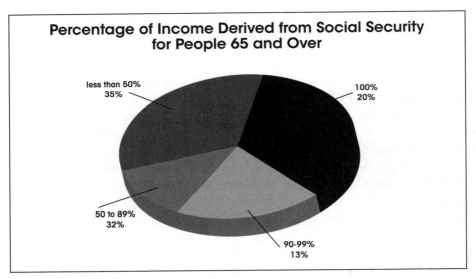

How clients perceive the value of a reverse mortgage is often a reflection of the financial reality from which they operate. Since, in order to even consider a reverse mortgage, a person must be at least 62, everyone eligible is a senior. However, that alone is far too big of a brush with which to paint the entire reverse mortgage market place. So, in order to understand what a reverse mortgage can do for clients, we must first determine from what perspective they are viewing the questions.

In effect, there are three possible positions from which a person 62 or older can consider whether or not a reverse mortgage is right for them.

The first group includes people who are faced with expenses that exceed their income. In these cases, the income that can be generated from a reverse mortgage can be used to meet (and hopefully exceed) their monthly expenses. This is the largest of the three groups we will cover here. You might be surprised as to just how big a block of seniors this group represents. According to data published in a report titled "65+ in the United States: 2005," published by the U.S. Department of Commerce in conjunction with the Department of Health and Human Services, when it comes to people over 65 years old, 97% cannot cover a check for $600 and 54% are still working, while only 3% are financially secure. Maybe the most disturbing thing of all is that bankruptcies among people 65 and over have increased by 164% in the last eight years!

For those in the group who have had the opportunity to do a reverse mortgage, it is hard to understand why they would not take advantage of it. Unfortunately, this is also the group least likely to get professional advice as they are often overlooked by financial planners because they might not fit the client profile of most planners.

The second group includes people who presently have enough income to meet their expenses, but have little or nothing left over. In these cases, the income that could be generated by a reverse mortgage can provide breathing room and relieve the anxiety many seniors suffer as a result of knowing they are one unexpected expense away from financial ruin. Many of these seniors may have financial advisors because they have assets: what makes them vulnerable is that their assets are stretched to their limits to produce the income they need to maintain their standard of living.

The last group includes those people with incomes that exceed their expenses. This is also the group that rarely considers even investigating reverse mortgages. There are a couple of reasons for this. The main one being that FHA-backed reverse mortgages were never designed for this group. Another is that the people in this group are largely unaware that there are private lenders who offer reverse mortgages that are not restricted by FHA lending limits. Lastly, and possibly the most overlooked reason is that they are unaware of the tax advantages they could capitalize on by using a reverse mortgage.

When it comes to "income," many planners fail to understand that the percentage of income seniors may receive from Social Security or some other government-related retirement plan has little to do with their total net worth.

On the other hand, what many couples fail to fully appreciate is the dramatic effect the loss of a spouse has on the household income. For years I have heard horror story after horror story about how a widow was left financially devastated because her husband took a 100% option on his pension. I am not sure why so many people opt for a few more dollars each month by betting on longevity, but they do.

Making the wrong decision about which option to choose with their pension fund distributions may only be one of the problems. For the most part, single and widowed seniors generally have much lower incomes than their married counterparts.

By learning about reverse mortgages earlier rather than later (or not at all), clients will not only be able to make informed decisions, but they will also have the opportunity to incorporate the alternative income options into their post-retirement planning.

A closer look at the disparity in income between couples and single seniors of both sexes reveals some issues most people never consider. In addition to the couple/single differences, there is also evidence that single women have lower income levels than senior single men.

Figure 4.2

Median Household Income

Married couples — Men living alone — Women living alone

	65+	65-69	70-74	75+
Married couples	$36,006	$45,305	$36,055	$29,280
Men living alone	$17,839	$17,842	$18,298	$16,937
Women living alone	$13,775	$16,474	$14,332	$13,172

Source: U.S. Department of Health and Human Services and U.S. Department of Commerce, "65+ in the United States, 2005"

Why Use a Reverse Mortgage?

CHAPTER 5

The reasons people choose to do a reverse mortgage are limited only by the number of people who do them. The most important thing to remember when considering a reverse mortgage is that the money being considered is in fact already the homeowner's money. As such, there is no need to justify how your clients intend to use their own money. This, however, does not alleviate the borrowers from the responsibility of thoroughly investigating and understanding how the reverse mortgage works and the effects it will have on their overall estate. In addition, we strongly suggest that would-be borrowers shop the marketplace in order to get the best deal for themselves.

The primary benefit of a reverse mortgage is that it allows people over 62 years old to retrieve a portion of the equity built up in their home. Although this is being done in the form of a loan, there is no requirement to make any repayments as long as the home serves as a primary residence for the borrower or, in joint cases, both borrowers. One of the most common concerns heard from people thinking about reverse mortgages is that they (or their heirs) could end up owing more than what the home sells for at the end of the mortgage. This is not the case. The mortgage insurance attached to the loan eliminates any liability for any portion of the loan that exceeds the sale price of the home even if the original appraisal price of the house depreciates. Not only is this a comfort while borrowers are living in the home and alive, it also provides comfort in knowing that their heirs and/or estate will never be liable for the repayment of any amount that might exceed the value received at the time of sale of the home.

Another important benefit deals with how income from a reverse mortgage is considered for tax purposes. The Internal Revenue Service does not consider the payments to be income, regardless as to how the payments are received. Nor are the funds received from HUD-approved mortgages taken into consideration for Medicare, Social Security, or other government benefits.

Most importantly, reverse mortgages can address two underestimated issues for retirees: "Personal Inflation" and "Dead Equity."

Aggregate vs. Personal Inflation

The longer people live after retirement, the more inflation becomes a critical component in their standard of living. As such, it is imperative that people living on retirement income understand and have a clear picture of inflation. To do this, we must make a distinction between aggregate inflation and personal inflation.

Aggregate inflation is the inflation figure with which we are most familiar. These figures are based on the Consumer Price Index (CPI). This index, however, is a national average that breaks down consumer expenditures in seven major categories. Unfortunately, it is rare that the CPI for any given year would be an actual reflection of the inflation rate a retired person in the United States would experience.

Personal inflation is another thing entirely: it reflects the actual inflation a person experiences based on those services and products he or she purchases and pays for in the normal course of living.

The following are two examples of how great the differences between aggregate and personal inflation can be: The first is in housing, where the average Consumer Price Index for housing is 42.3% of the household income. For many retired people (particularly those who have their houses paid off) that percentage would be significantly lower. The second example would be medical care. The average person in America has a Consumer Price Index of 6.2% for medical expenses. Many retired people find that their medical expenses can be 20% to 40% (or possibly even higher percentages) of their total expenditures.

So, it is of little surprise that people who have been retired for any length of time will tell you that personal inflation is much more important to them than an aggregate inflation figure. Unfortunately, benefits such as Social Security and pension increases are based on aggregate percentages. As such, having a pool of money from which to tap for increased expenses resulting from personal inflation makes the reverse mortgage option very attractive.

As advisors to retired clients, it is imperative that we consider all the facts that can erode their income as well as their asset base. I have attached the following graph that illustrates how income declines for married and single individuals as they get older, which result in their need to make withdrawals from their core assets.

Figure 5.1

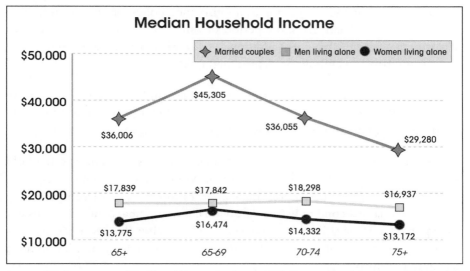

Source: U.S. Department of Health and Human Services and U.S. Department of Commerce, "65+ in the United States: 2005"

Dead Equity

This brings us to the concept I like to refer to as "dead equity." Before the significance of dead equity can be understood, it must first be properly framed within the scope of an overall portfolio. For the most part, portfolios are made up of equities, bonds, real estate equity, collectibles, insurance and annuities, cash, and/or any private business ownership. The combined value of all of these make up an individual's net worth. With the exception of cash, all of the these items are subject to market value, which means regardless of what we may think they are worth, their true value when liquidated is entirely dependent on how much someone in the marketplace is willing to pay for them at any specific time.

Another point that we need to take into consideration is how long it takes to convert any of these items into cash at any given time. Cash, of course, is always liquid. Savings accounts and certificates of deposit are extremely liquid as they can be converted upon request. Stocks and bonds are considered highly liquid because they are bought and sold within the framework of exchanges that dictate that not only can we sell them, but we can also expect to receive the cash within a specific period, generally a few days.

The cash values of life insurance and annuities are also considered to be highly liquid. Although the actual amount of time this takes can vary from company to company, converting a life insurance policy or annuity into cash can be done in a relatively short period of time. In addition, state insurance departments provide us with additional safeguards for these products that require companies to follow predetermined guidelines.

When it comes to liquidating collectibles and ownership in private businesses, the size of the marketplace in which they operate affects not only the time it takes but also what a buyer might be willing to pay for them.

Real estate, on the other hand, particularly primary residences, often hold a unique position in a person's net worth. More often than not, a person's home represents his or her largest single asset. In most cases, where it is not the largest it is usually second only to an individual retirement account. To consider the equity in a home as liquid would be a mistake. Why? Because not only does it take a long period of time to convert into cash, the equity in a home has a zero rate of return.

The reason we consider it "dead equity" is because the homeowner cannot access these funds without either selling the home (which, of course, results in the need for another place to live) or by creating a debt that requires not only the repayment of principal but also of interest. Since few seniors are interested in acquiring the additional monthly payments generated by accessing the equity within their home through the use of traditional mortgages or equity lines of credit, they generally find these alternatives unattractive.

In addition, even if a person was interested in purchasing a new home and using the proceeds from a former home to buy the new residence, it would not change the status of his equity position. The equity simply moved from one residence to another. To retired people, home equity is a lot like having a gold mine on a deserted island—it is nice to have and it certainly increases their net worth, but it really does not do them much good.

Underused equity in the homes of retired persons may be considered a large part of their overall net worth but really has little intrinsic value. In short,

I have come to the conclusion that dead equity can best be described as that portion of retired people's assets tied up in the equity of their home that in reality is an underperforming asset.

The following chart is one I created: the data used to generate this chart is based on the results of over 100 interviews I conducted with retired people while researching this book.

Figure 5.2

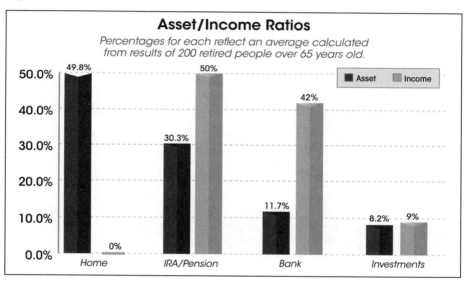

Another reason I call it "dead equity" is that for some reason almost all seniors who own their homes intend to leave those homes to their children or heirs. Who, in turn, are going to sell the home, thus converting the equity into cash. I find this interesting because when I was interviewing seniors for this book I would ask what they planned to do with their homes. Almost everyone said they intended to leave their homes to their kids. When I followed that question by asking which of their children did they think would move in, they almost all answered that they did not think any of their children would ever even consider living in their houses.

In short, the only people who would ever benefit from the cash built up in their homes would be their children after they are dead, which, of course, is an entirely different way to define dead equity.

This is where a forward-thinking financial planner might want to bring up the idea of a reverse mortgage. It will allow a senior to access a portion of the equity without requiring any repayment of any kind as long as the property remains the senior's primary residence.

Now, this does not mean that there is not going to be any interest charged or repayment of principal required. What it means is that you have created a loan that allows them to defer all payments until such time as the borrower or both borrowers no longer live in that residence or have passed away.

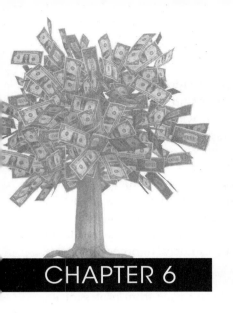

Is a Reverse Mortgage Right for Your Client?

CHAPTER 6

For the most part, it is safe to assume that clients make decisions for their own reasons. Whether those reasons make sense to other people usually does not play a big role in their thinking. Why should we not expect this rule to hold true when it comes to whether someone decides to take out a reverse mortgage? After all, it is a personal decision and, as such, the reason for doing it will be different from person to person. In some cases, the need for this additional money is the deciding factor; while, in others, these funds provide the borrowers with opportunities they would otherwise not have in their golden years. For those who are fortunate enough to find themselves in a comfortable financial position, using tax-free money from a reverse mortgage can provide them with tax-reduction benefits. Whatever the reason clients do or do not take out a loan on their home equity, the fact reminds that a reverse mortgage is nothing more than a tool that can be used to unlock cash that has built up in equity. And since this equity does belong to the homeowners, how they use it is their business.

I have talked to a number people who have used reverse mortgages. Their reasons for doing so ranged from those that I found logical to others that made no sense to me whatsoever. As stated prior, the only important thing is that the reverse mortgage makes sense to the borrower.

With this in mind, I almost always suggest to clients considering a reverse mortgage that they take the time to think about what they are doing by completing a little exercise designed to help them focus. This exercise is made up of the following nine-step process:

(1) **Education:** like almost every financial decision clients face in their lives, having a thorough understanding of how a reverse mortgage works, what costs and fees are associated with establishing a reverse mortgage, and how it will affect the rest of their portfolio is of great importance.

Although clients can rely on others to provide them with this information, the only way to ensure that they are making the right decision is by thoroughly investigating the process. There are numerous information resources available from both the government and the private sector from which they can draw in order to educate themselves.

While they should not hesitate in seeking advice from professionals, decisions should be made based on the information they have uncovered rather than relying on others.

(2) **Defining the need:** when we talk about defining a need for reverse mortgages, what we are saying is that it is important to explore the opportunities a reverse mortgage may provide and it is always more prudent to have a well-defined need for the money before starting to shop for a reverse mortgage.

By defining a need first, your clients provide themselves with the opportunity to not only thoroughly consider their objectives, but also to do some planning that will enable them to come up with a realistic amount of money they want and in what form they wish to take those funds.

(3) **Proper placement and effect of a reverse mortgage funds on their estate:** if there is one area that is more often overlooked than any other when clients are looking at a reverse mortgage, it is the effect that the new inflow of cash will have on their overall asset base and/or estate plan.

If clients are going to do a reverse mortgage to make a one-time purchase such as motor home, a dream vacation, or even paying for the wedding or college of their grandchildren, the effect of the cash they receive will, in reality, have little consequence when it comes to their daily living expenses.

If, on the other hand, they take their monthly payment to supplement their income and transfer some other lump sum of money from a taxable to a tax-free or tax-deferred status, this transaction will almost always affect the amount of income tax they pay on an annual basis.

The fact remains that any influx of cash (whether it be on a small monthly basis or a large one-time, lump-sum deposit) will have an effect on their financial plan and most likely on their estate plan. It is the reason clients should discuss the ramifications of using a reverse mortgage with their financial planner as well as their accountant.

(4) **Mandatory counseling:** in order to qualify for the federally-insured Home Equity Conversion Mortgage (HECM—more commonly referred to as an FHA reverse mortgage) clients must first meet with and discuss the process with a counselor employed by a nonprofit or public agency approved by HUD.

HUD considers this counseling to be one of the most important consumer protections built into its reverse mortgage program. The intent of the counseling is to ensure that clients understand the program and have a chance to review and ask questions about alternative options before they ever apply for reverse mortgage.

Though this process is required for federally-backed reverse mortgages, it is not always the case when your clients are dealing strictly with the private sector. However, regardless of what lender your clients decide to use, they should see this requirement as a positive step and take full advantage of the counseling service. They should probably not meet with a counselor until they have done their homework and can go to that meeting with any and all questions they have about the process, how it works, and all of the fees and costs associated with a reverse mortgage.

(5) **Choosing a mortgage company:** choosing the mortgage company to use to write a reverse mortgage is almost assuredly going to be the most important decision your client will make during the entire process. In many cases, the federally-backed reverse mortgages done through a mortgage company backed by their local FHA office will be the way to go. However, there are numerous factors that may make the choice of a private mortgage company more advantageous in particular situations.

The only way your clients can ensure that they choose the best system is to shop multiple reverse mortgage lenders and compare what is being offered at what cost and on what terms.

It does not cost anything to get quotes from many different companies. After doing an initial review, your clients can generally narrow down which two or three different companies would be best for them. After which, it is more than worth their time to meet with and listen to the presentations of representatives from these different companies.

Although many people find this too tedious and time-consuming, the fact remains that it is the only way to ensure that your clients are choosing the mortgage company that best meets their needs.

(6) **Choosing a distribution method:** the distribution method your clients select is also a critical decision that must be made at the beginning of the process. Although most companies offer three methods to choose from (lump sum, monthly payment, and a line of credit), there are some that may offer only two choices. Each distribution method has its advantages and drawbacks. Before deciding on which type of payout system to choose, your clients should give thorough consideration to all three, and keep in mind that whenever possible flexibility is a value within itself.

The method that offers the most flexibility is a line of credit. The main drawback of the line of credit method, when compared to the monthly payment method, is that the line of credit has a preset amount of money available to the borrower. Whereas, with the monthly payment method, they can receive money for as long as they live, regardless of the percentage the loan represents of the property (which includes both principal and interest). In theory, a person who chooses the monthly payment method could end up receiving money in excess of the value of the property.

When compared to the lump-sum method, the total amount available through the line of credit method will almost always be less than the amount of the one-time payment your client could receive under the lump-sum method.

Each situation dictates its own set of priorities and personal situations need to be paramount in any decision as to which method to choose.

(7) **The application process:** this process is dictated by the mortgage company chosen to do the reverse mortgage. In addition, the actual time it takes to complete the process will differ from company to company. So, rather than going in with preconceived notions as to what should happen when, we suggest that clients go over the process when interviewing the lenders.

By understanding all the requirements the company has for reverse mortgages and making sure that your clients' expectations have been communicated should avoid or minimize delays, unforeseen costs, and general frustration.

(8) **Who needs to know?** This is an interesting question, as for the most part, clients do not think their children (or anybody else for that matter) are entitled to know what the clients do with their money. Money is still (as before) an uncomfortable subject to talk about with others. Most clients do not feel they have an obligation to explain to their children how they have invested or intend to spend their future inheritance.

Having said that, consideration must be given to the unusual change that comes over so many retired people. For some reason, many retirees think they have to explain and justify their actions when it comes to their assets with their children. What is even more remarkable is the number of cases where clients are doing things because their children want to access their inheritance while the parents are still alive. This is, of course, an entirely different topic in itself and could generate hundreds of hundreds of pages in another book. It does point out, however, that, in many cases, the parents do want to discuss the effects of the reverse mortgage on their home and how that would be treated after their death. As to whether or not the children agree with their decision, which in reality should be of little to no relevance, in spite of this it is often a major component of the decision as to whether or not to do a reverse mortgage, regardless of any benefits.

For those clients who feel their children should be involved in this decision, their children should meet with their parents' financial planner in order to address all the issues the children feel are relevant. In effect, there is no good answer to this but it is something that must be addressed in the process.

(9) **Exit strategies:** like any financial decision or business decision, part of the planning process should include an exit strategy. With reverse mortgages (although limited) there are strategies that should be considered. The first, of course, being that the loan will be settled when the owner vacates the house permanently or has passed away. This is the exit strategy in most cases.

Another possible exit strategy is repayment of the loan in full while the owner still lives on the premises and prior to death.

Still another strategy would be for the heirs of the retirees to use other funds either from the estate itself or from their own assets to purchase the property at the time the loan is due.

While talking about exit strategies, consider that the children (or some other family member, friend, or associate) may want to do a private reverse mortgage with the property owner. Although this does not have the safeguards or security that one gets from an FHA or other private reverse mortgage, it does open the door for a different approach. Of course, the exit strategy here is that the person or persons making the payments to the homeowner would stop doing so, and the two parties would settle the loan.

In some cases, this is a very viable option, particularly for those situations where multiple children are involved. If one or more of the parties involved want to purchase the home, they can do so by paying off the balance of the loan and giving those not interested in any future ownership of the property cash. Like any exit strategy, there are pros and cons that need to be taken into consideration.

(10) **Closing:** the closing of a reverse mortgage is very much the same as the closing of a traditional mortgage; it is the final meeting where all the parties gather and all the paperwork is signed, and money changes hands.

Just like in a traditional mortgage, the closing of a reverse mortgage is never a good time for new items or changes to be introduced. Any questions about a reverse mortgage should have been answered before getting to the closing. Any new information brought to the attention of clients at closing that were not provided prior to the closing should be seen as a huge red flag. There should be no surprises or changes in the contract, the interest rate, or the amount of money available to the clients. Again, just like a traditional mortgage, there is nothing wrong with clients taking a legal adviser to this close.

If (for whatever reason) the agreement expected is different from the one presented at closing, there is absolutely nothing wrong with clients putting a stop to the proceedings until all questions are answered and all concerns satisfactorily addressed.

Remember, the purpose of closing is to bring to an end the process of establishing the reverse mortgage—to terminate any negotiations as to terms and conditions. Even though clients retain the "Right of Recession" for three business days after closing, they should go into the closing with all their questions answered and all their concerns addressed to their satisfaction with intent to complete the contract.

Reverse Mortgage Examples

As financial planners, it is imperative that we keep in mind that our role in the reverse mortgage arena is one of an advisor. This advisory role should never be one of saying "yes" or "no" but rather one that addresses issues from an educational point of view.

In other words, we should never say "do" or "don't do," but rather give our clients information that reflects how their decision will affect their portfolios. As such, you may be faced with a situation where you think the clients' plans for the money they get from a reverse mortgage are ridiculous. The fact is that it is their money and what they want to do with is not really any of your business. What is your business is how taking that money affects the funds you manage. If the money received from a reverse mortgage does not have any effect on their financial plan, then that should be what you tell them.

In short, your professional position is that of an educator, not a judge.

The following are some examples of how people have used reverse mortgages to accomplish goals.

Mary Ann Finally Gets to Retire at 74

Mary Ann and her husband, George, had retired the same year and had been retired for a little over four years when George suddenly, and unexpectedly, died from a heart attack.

They were both receiving Social Security and had a little over $200,000 in savings, but the majority of their retirement income came from George's company pension plan. Unfortunately, George chose a 100% payout based on his life only, rather than a spousal benefit payout. As a result, at George's death, Mary Ann was no longer entitled to any additional payments from George's retirement plan. What she thought would be a comfortable retirement suddenly became a financial disaster.

So, at 69 years of age, Mary Ann went back to work. She made just a little over minimum wage, but it was enough to maintain her lifestyle. As time went by, Mary Ann became more and more depressed. Not only was the leisurely retirement she had dreamed of for so many years now gone, it was becoming physically harder for her to maintain her work schedule.

Then, someone told her about reverse mortgages. Mary Ann had never had much experience dealing with money, but she went to her local FHA office and was able to get through the process with little difficulty. Finally, at the age of 74, Mary Ann was able to retire. She now receives a guaranteed monthly income that not only allowed her to stop working, but it also provides her with more than enough money to maintain her lifestyle, with a few perks every month.

David and Kathy Finally Go on that Cross Country Vacation

Like a lot of people, David and Kathy had always dreamed about taking a long, leisurely trip across the United States in a motor home. It was something they always had wanted to do as soon after they retired as possible, while they would still have enough stamina and energy to explore the entire country.

Shortly after retiring, they came to the sad realization that although they could more than likely live comfortably for the rest of their lives, they did not have the extra money needed to buy or rent a motor home for prolonged trips, let alone the money needed to cover the ever-increasing cost of gas it would take to make these trips. In short, their long-time dreams of care-free traveling were in fact financially unfeasible.

It was then that they started thinking about using a reverse mortgage. This would provide them with the lump-sum cash they needed to not only purchase a motor home, but also provide them with more than enough money to pay for all the expenses they would incur on what they were planning to be a nine-month trip.

After completing the paperwork for the reverse mortgage, they received a credit line with a maximum limit of $156,000, of which they used $102,000 to purchase a motor home. Rather than going on one nine-month trip, they were able to make two six-month trips over the next three years. Since that time, they have used their motor home for numerous shorter trips to visit their children and friends on a number of occasions.

Though many people would not consider buying a motor home a wise way to use a reverse mortgage, Dave and Kathy think it is one of the best decisions they have ever made. They are thoroughly enjoying their retirement and believe their motor home has played a large part in their contentment.

Bill Remodels Their Home for Nancy

Bill was 75 when his wife, Nancy, whom he had been married to for 52 years, had a debilitating stroke at the age of 73. Although Nancy was clearheaded and her mind as sharp as ever, doctors informed Bill that she would be wheelchair-bound for the remainder of her life.

Determined that he would do everything in his power to make her life as comfortable as possible, and knowing the Nancy loved the house they had lived in for the last 24 years, Bill immediately started looking into how to make the house wheelchair-accessible. Widening doorways and adding ramps would not prove to be a major problem. What was problematic was all four bedrooms were on the second floor of the house. The solution seemed apparent—convert their large, two-car garage into a new master bedroom suite and, while doing so, put in a wheelchair-accessible bathroom. Not so apparent, however, was where to find the capital needed for such major renovations. Both Bill and Nancy agreed that this was necessary, regardless of the cost, which meant they needed to come up with $133,000.

They had three choices: they could take the entire amount from their savings, they could take out an equity line of credit, or they could do a reverse mortgage. Although they had the money in their savings, they did not feel comfortable using this as it had always provided them with a sense of security. Using an equity line of credit was certainly an option, but Bill did not like the idea of incurring any additional monthly payments. This left them with a reverse mortgage, which after comparing with the other two, they decided was their best option.

Taking Care of Those Nagging Daily Expenses

Renée had been a schoolteacher for 43 years when she retired at the end of the school year in 1982 at the age of 65. By 2007, she was 80 years old, still healthy, still working in the garden, still volunteering at her church, and still very active in her local senior women's group. Her problem was that over the years, inflation had slowly eroded the savings she had set aside to be used as a supplement to her retirement benefits and in case of emergency. Now that this money was needed, she came to the sad conclusion that not only would it not be enough to supplement her retirement should any emergency arise, but such an emergency would most likely wipe out all of her savings at once. In an effort to figure out how she might be able to cut back on expenditures, Mary decided to take a look at her monthly expenses. She was dumbfounded. Those everyday items she had purchased in 1992 for $100 now, in 2007, cost her $265. And although she was very thrifty, the income she received from her pension and Social Security in no way kept up with the increased inflation of her lifestyle. Renée was now facing a cold reality that many retirees face—even though she had always saved, she had not planned well. She used certificates of deposit as her sole savings vehicle, because she always thought that 100% safety was the most important thing. What she did not realize was that certificates of deposit are by their nature low-interest, highly-taxable, short-term savings vehicles. As a result, after taxes and inflation she had in fact lost money over the years.

Then, one day one of her friends told her about reverse mortgages. The teacher in her came out and she spent the next two weeks thoroughly researching reverse mortgages. After coming to the conclusion that this was in fact a very viable option for her, Renée took a closer look and decided that a reverse mortgage was right for her. She took out a loan in the form of a $164,000 line of credit that easily replaced the funds she had lost to taxes and inflation. Renée has no intention of using all of this line-of-credit, but it does provide her with a lot of comfort, knowing that she has ready access to money if and when she needs it.

Reverse Mortgages and Long-Term Care

The advantage of employing a reverse mortgage when dealing with the issue of long-term care coverage is very straightforward; yet, for whatever reason, many people in need of long-term care insurance coverage seem confused as to how this relationship can work.

The advantage of using a reverse mortgage or at least some of the income derived from a reverse mortgage is that it will allow clients to purchase long-term care insurance, or continue to pay for a long-term care insurance policy that is already in force. For years, people in the long-term care insurance industry have heard from clients and agents that one of the largest stumbling blocks they face with long-term care planning is that clients cannot find the money needed to pay the premiums. By using a reverse mortgage that problem is often easily solved. Consider that those people who do not have long-term care insurance in place are in fact subjecting their homes to the Recovery Act. The idea of using a reverse mortgage to pay for long-term care insurance makes even more sense.

Like almost every other situation faced when dealing with personal finance, advanced planning is the key. As such, anyone who is least 62 and is doing long-term care planning should at least look at a reverse mortgage as a possible solution for providing the premiums needed to maintain a long-term-care insurance policy. If for whatever reason they cannot qualify for long-term care insurance, a reverse mortgage should be given at least some consideration as an option should long-term care services ever be needed.

In either case, when it comes to long-term care, the very least a reverse mortgage can do is offer alternatives that should be considered.

Using Reverse Mortgages to Reduce Taxes

For many retired seniors who depend on interest earned from taxable vehicles (such as certificates of deposit, Fannie Maes, personal mortgages, and corporate bonds) as a primary source of income, a reverse mortgage offers alternatives that can have dramatic and positive effects on the amount of taxes they pay. An example of this would be Mary who is a 72-year-old woman with an annual income of $51,065. Her annual income is broken down as follows: 18,000 from Social Security, $16,565 from interest she earns on a certificate of deposit, and $16,500 she receives in distributions from an IRA.

The income generated by the interest on the certificate of deposit and the distributions from the IRA are subject to federal income tax. Although the money she receives from Social Security represents about a third of her total income, only a portion of it is taxable. See Chapter 10 for more details.

And even though there is nothing she could do to change the tax status of the $16,500 she receives from her IRA, it may be possible to reduce the amount of tax she pays by repositioning other assets into a tax-deferred positions. It is the taxable money she is receiving from the CDs that provide her with an opportunity to reduce her taxes and increase her spendable income. Mary can use a reverse mortgage to replace the money she is receiving from the CD. Although the dollar amount would be the same, the amount she saves by not having to pay taxes on the income generated from the reverse mortgage and moving the funds she has in certificates of deposit into tax-deferred or tax-exempt vehicles will not only increase her spendable income, but, also reduce her overall tax. By doing this, Mary may also be able to reduce the taxable amount of her Social Security benefits. It is the tax-free nature of the funds generated from a reverse mortgage that provides her with this opportunity.

Summary

These few examples don't begin to cover all the endless reasons people have used to do reverse mortgages, but they will give you an idea of the thought processes used. This brings us once again to our primary question; why should a financial planner play a role in the reverse mortgage discussion process?

The establishment of a reverse mortgage generates a new source of tax-free cash that cannot help but make a difference in the borrower's current financial situation. This is where the financial planner comes in; the planner can help the borrower best put to use this new source of money, and in order to do this the entire portfolio must be taken into consideration. Even though most reverse mortgage programs require some sort of financial counseling, it is highly unlikely that these counselors will fully understand the structure of a senior's entire portfolio or the reasons it was set up the way it was. Here is where the expertise and professionalism of a financial planner comes in to play.

Financial planners will also understand that the primary benefit to be gained from a reverse mortgage is providing the homeowner with the opportunity to generate a source of easily accessible, tax-free cash on a recurring basis as an income stream, or to provide a large lump sum of money, or to generate a line of credit. Once again, financial planners can prove to be an asset as they can give the options as to which of these three methods of distribution will most benefit their client. By taking into consideration all aspects of their clients' portfolio, financial planners can suggest the most appropriate use of these funds, which may affect and dramatically change both the income and the growth aspects of the borrower's portfolio.

In reality, there appears to be no limit in the number of different reasons people have used a reverse mortgage.

We have all read and heard about cases where people have taken out reverse mortgages to go on vacations, to pay for weddings *(their own, their children's and even their grandchildren's)*, pay college tuition as well as other educational expenses, to buy boats, cars, trucks and motorcycles, invest in small businesses, or provide cash influx for businesses of their children, other family members, or even friends. We have even talked to one gentleman who used the funds from his reverse mortgage to buy a plane, and another who used the funds to buy model trains.

The interesting thing here is that the only people that need to be satisfied with the reasons they are using a reverse mortgage are the people who are applying for the reverse mortgage.

What to Expect in an Actual Reverse Mortgage Proposal

CHAPTER 8

The purpose of this section is to provide information on what should be looked at in a quote when considering which reverse mortgage company best meets the borrower's needs.

After receiving quotes, it is imperative that the quotes be read and studied until all the fees, charges, and costs associated with the generation of the quotes are understood. It is recommended that the company representatives are called and asked to explain every aspect of their proposal. The information package received from the reverse mortgage company should include information about the company, the FHC/HECM page (which provides a program summary), a brochure that addresses general questions, an Estimated Amortization Schedule, a Benefits Summary, and a Good Faith Estimate, along with the business card of the contact person.

Although all the information the company provides should be reviewed and understood, the Estimated Amortization Schedule, Good Faith Estimate, and Benefits Summary are of special importance because they in fact provide a view of the working components of the mortgage.

Start with the Benefits Summary. Do not be side-tracked with the Good Faith Estimate, which will provide an itemized listing of the costs of generating and maintaining the mortgage, or be caught up in the complexities of an Estimated Amortization Schedule without first being sure and comfortable with the overall view provided by the Benefits Summary.

Benefits Summary: The Benefits Summary should include the name and number of the person originating the loan, usually but not always referred to as the loan advisor. It should also include the borrower's name. It is also important check to insure the date of birth is correct, keeping in mind that if it is a joint mortgage, the date of birth reflected would be that of the younger person.

One of the most important parts of the Benefits Summary is the line that requires the borrower's signature. Signing and returning this page indicates that the borrower has not only reviewed but more importantly understood this summary page. It is strongly suggested that the time be taken to understand every line on this form, regardless of how long it takes. It is also a good idea to get any questions answered by people that understand reverse mortgages, people other than the loan originator.

The following is an example of a Benefits Summary received from a reverse mortgage company. For the purpose of putting it this book I have altered its layout but not its contents.

There are 19 different items listed. Note that only three of these items have any explanation. It is important to understand the other 16 items as well. The other items are explained below.

Estimated Closing Date: This is the target date for the closing of the loan. Generally the date found in the Benefits Summary will be 30 days from the date the Benefits Summary is generated. Keep in mind that the lending company and loan broker only get paid after the loan has closed. This is proper and there is absolute nothing wrong with this; however, it is in their best interest to close a loan as soon as possible. On the other hand, the borrower's best interest is what should be paramount in this process. As such, we always suggest that borrowers take whatever amount of time they need to ensure that they not only understand the reverse mortgage but also believe it is in fact the right thing for them. Having said this, it is also important to emphasize that regardless as to what financial payments are chosen (a lump sum, line of credit, or a set monthly payment), no funds will be transferred to the borrower until after the mortgage is closed.

Figure 8.1 – Benefits Summary

Benefits Summary

HECM Monthly

Your Loan Advisor: *Named deliberately omitted*

Phone: *Number deliberately omitted*   **Borrower Name:** John Sanderson

Estimated Date of Closing	12/13/2007	
Youngest Borrower DOB	12/09/1940	Youngest Borrower's Age: 67
Expected Interest Rate	5.890%	
Margin	1.500%	
Initial Interest Rate	5.430%	
Lending Limit	$252,890.00	
Property Appraised Value	$300,000.00	
Maximum Claim Amount	$252,890.00	
Principal Limit	$157,550.47	
IMIP	$5,067.80	
Origination Fee	$5,057.24	
Other Closing Costs	$4,016.24	
Initial Draw	$0.00	
Liens	$0.00	
Servicing Set-Aside	$4,972.38	Monthly Servicing Fee: $30
Net Principal Limit	$138,446.25	
Line of Credit	$138,446.25	Initial Growth Rate: 5.930%
Monthly Payments	$0.00	
Length of Term	Line of Credit	

John Sanderson   Date

Expected Interest Rate: This is the average of the interest rates mortgages have been issued at over the past ten years. As such, it is highly unlikely that the expected interest rate that is listed on a Benefits Summary will be the actual interest rate used.

Margin: This is the difference (spread) between the actual rate you will be charged and the current Treasury bill rate.

Initial Interest Rate: This is the rate your loan is projected to be made at; however, it is only an estimate and the actual rate may be different.

Lending Limit: This is the maximum amount the mortgage company is willing to make on the property.

Property Appraised Value: This is the value placed on the property by an approved appraiser.

Maximum Claim Amount: This is the lesser of the appraised value or the lending limit.

Principal Limit: This is the maximum amount of any loan the FHA will approve.

IMIP: This is the insurance that covers any contingencies. The first being that borrowers will receive more in monthly payments over their lifetime than the value of their house when it is sold after their death. This insures the heirs that the reverse mortgage will never make claims on the estate greater than the value of the home at the borrowers' death. The second contingency is to insure the lending company from loss in case the sale of the property does not cover the total of payments made during the life of the loan.

Origination Fee: This is the fee charged by the lender to prepare the loan, which includes but is not limited to the administrative costs, marketing expenses, and commissions.

Other Closing Costs: This is the total of all the charges and fees associated with the loan and paid at the settlement or closing of the loan. This cost can be found in an itemized form on the Good Faith Estimate.

Initial Draw: If more than one method of receiving the funds is used, the amount that is received at closing (really 3 days after closing) is the Initial Withdrawal. Example: If the Net Amount is $50,000 and the borrower wanted

$20,000 in a lump sum at closing and $30,000 left in a Line of Credit, $20,000 would be the Initial Withdrawal.

Servicing Set-Aside: This is a dollar figure that is set-aside in the equity of the loan; it is not a charge to the borrower, but it does reduce the total amount available to the borrower. This figure is generated by multiplying the monthly service fee by the borrower's life expectancy. In this case, the $4,972.38 represents 165.7 months or 13.8 years. This is the borrower's life expectancy according to the Lender. This represents the total of the monthly servicing fees expected over the life of the loan, which the FHA requires the Lender to subtract from the Principal Limit. In this case, it reduces the Principal Limit from $157,550.47 to $152,578.09. This may sound confusing and it probably should. We have never received what we consider a satisfactory explanation from any Lender or HUD.

Net Principal Limit: This is the amount of credit available after all fees, charges, and set-asides have been subtracted from the Principal Limit.

Line of Credit: This is a predetermined sum of money that can be accessed as desired by the borrower at different times and for different amounts as long as the total amount borrowed does not exceed the original predetermined sum. Once a borrower has a line of credit in place, there is no limit as to how or when they can access the funds.

Having a line of credit provides borrowers with maximum flexibility, as they have access to the entire amount available but can determine how much, how often, and for what reasons they access the funds. The amount of interest that accumulates on a line of credit is based on the outstanding balance borrowed at any given time charged. As such, the line of credit may be $150,000 but if the borrower withdraws only $10,000, interest will only be accumulating on the $10,000 rather than $150,000. The advantages of having a large sum of money available and being able to access small or large portions at any specific times provides borrowers with a great deal of flexibility.

Of the three methods available for withdrawing money from reverse mortgage, the line of credit method provides the most flexibility. Unlike the lump-sum method where a large sum, usually the maximum limit, is taken out at once and interest starts to accumulate immediately, the line of credit method provides borrowers with the access to the maximum amount allowable but also provides borrowers with the flexibility to withdraw smaller amounts as needed or desired. One of the advantages here is that interest is only accumulating on the amount of money that has been accessed rather than the total amount. The monthly payment method provides a preset amount of money that is paid monthly either for life or for a set period of time. The line of credit method can also be used on a monthly basis, but it allows the monthly amount to be increased, decreased, or even stopped at any given time. And once stopped, additional funds can be withdrawn periodically as they are needed or desired by the borrower.

Length of Term: This refers to the type of loan being made (that is, a lump-sum, line-of-credit or monthly payment), how long that will be available, and at what time payment will be required.

The Good Faith Estimate: This page should include an itemized listing of the all the fees and charges accumulated in the generation and required for the maintenance of the mortgage. In addition, it should include the name and address of the reverse mortgage company as well as the name of the representative making the proposal, and the phone and fax numbers for both. In addition, it should state the appraised property value, the maximum claim amount, the initial interest rate, the youngest applicant's age, and the estimated closing date. All of which should be identical to the corresponding numbers, percentages, and closing date on the Benefits Summary.

The following is an example of a Good Faith Estimate that was requested and received from a reverse mortgage company. For the purpose of putting it in this book, I have altered its layout but not its contents.

In this sample, the Appraised Property Value is $300,000, the Maximum Claim Amount is $252,890 and the initial Interest Rate is 5.43%.

At the bottom of a Good Faith Estimate will be found a signature line for both the borrower and the lender representative. More importantly, a disclosure statement, which states that the charges and fees stated are only estimates and that they may be more or less than those applied at settlement, should also be found. Now these numbers should correspond with those contained in the HUD-1 Settlement Statement that the borrower will receive at settlement, which show the actual cost for all items the borrower is responsible for paying. The last thing is a disclosure notification *(usually in bold font)* stating that this is a Good Faith Estimate and NOT a loan commitment.

Figure 8.2 – Good Faith Estimate

Good Faith Estimate			
Charges	Lender Paid	Borrower Paid	Total Paid
Loan Origination Fee	$0.00	$5,057.80	$5,057.80
Appraisal Fee	$0.00	$400.00	$400.00
Credit Report	$0.00	$12.00	$12.00
Flood Certificate	$0.00	$10.00	$10.00
MIP	$0.00	$5,057.80	$5,057.80
Settlement or Closing Fee	$0.00	$395.00	$395.00
Title Examination	$0.00	$150.00	$150.00
Title Insurance Binder	$0.00	$50.00	$50.00
Document Preparation Fee	$0.00	$125.00	$125.00
Attorney's Fees	$0.00	$450.00	$450.00
Title Insurance	$0.00	$632.23	$632.23
Deed Recording Fees	$0.00	$85.00	$85.00
Mortgage Recording Fees	$0.00	$589.00	$589.00
Deed City/County Tax Stamps	$0.00	$1,138.01	$1,138.01
Total Fees	$0.00	$14,131.84	$14,131.84

Since the lender is requiring the borrowers to pay every cost associated with the reverse mortgage, including their attorney fees, I suggest every line on this page be considered as a negotiation point. I also suggest that any commitment from the lender be in writing and that it agrees to cover any costs at closing that are in excess of what is listed on this Good Faith Estimate. Keep in mind that the borrower is being asked to pay a lot of money, in this case $14,131.84 before ever receiving a penny in any form. Another way to think about it is that the borrower has accumulated fees at a rate of 8.97% on the $157,550.47 Principal Amount or 5.59% of the Maximum Claim Amount. Either way you calculate it, it adds up to a lot of money. Remember there are plenty of companies out there competing for the borrower's business and the only time to negotiate the best deal is before closing on the mortgage. One of the best ways to go about this is to gather multiple quotes from different reverse mortgage companies licensed to operate in the state.

The last spreadsheet needed to be reviewed is the **Amortization Schedule Estimate**, which once again is only an estimate. The reason for an Amortization Schedule is to provide you with a snap shot of the status of your loan over time. However, since the components that make up these schedules are variable rather than fixed and will most likely fluctuate from year to year, these schedules are in reality of limited use. They will however provide the borrower with the actual interest rate being charged in any given year. It is interesting to note that the expected interest rate listed on every proposal we have received during our research for this book has in fact been less than the actual rate listed on the accompanying Amortization Schedules.

The following has been generated from the Estimated Amortization Schedule that accompanied the above Benefit Summary and Good Faith Estimate, with the assumptions of an expected interest rate of 5.890% and an appreciation of 4% on the property. There is also a monthly service charge for maintaining the loan of $30 for the first 17 years.

Figure 8.3 – Estimated Amortization Schedule

Assumes and Expect Interest rate of 5.890 and Home Price Appreciation of 4%

Yr	Age	Available Credit	Starting Balance	Borrower Payments	Service Charges	Accrued MIP	Accrued MIP	Ending Balance	Property Value	Retained Equity
1	67	$146,883	$14,132	$ –	$360	$74	$869	$15,434	$312,000	$296,566
2	68	$155,834	$15,434	$ –	$360	$80	$948	$16,823	$324,480	$307,657
3	69	$165,330	$16,823	$ –	$360	$88	$1,032	$18,303	$337,459	$319,157
4	70	$175,405	$18,303	$ –	$360	$95	$1,122	$19,880	$350,958	$331,078
5	71	$186,094	$19,880	$ –	$360	$103	$1,218	$21,561	$364,996	$343,435
6	72	$197,434	$21,561	$ –	$360	$112	$1,319	$23,352	$379,596	$356,244
7	73	$209,466	$23,352	$ –	$360	$121	$1,428	$25,262	$394,780	$369,518
8	74	$222,230	$25,262	$ –	$360	$131	$1,544	$27,297	$410,571	$383,274
9	75	$235,773	$27,297	$ –	$360	$142	$1,667	$29,466	$426,994	$397,528
10	76	$250,140	$29,466	$ –	$360	$153	$1,799	$31,777	$444,073	$412,296
11	77	$265,383	$31,777	$ –	$360	$165	$1,939	$34,241	$461,836	$427,595
12	78	$281,556	$34,241	$ –	$360	$177	$2,089	$36,867	$480,310	$443,443
13	79	$298,713	$36,867	$ –	$360	$191	$3,248	$39,666	$499,522	$459,856
14	80	$316,916	$39,666	$ –	$360	$205	$2,418	$42,649	$519,503	$476,854
15	81	$336,229	$42,649	$ –	$360	$221	$2,599	$45,828	$540,283	$494,455
16	82	$356,718	$45,828	$ –	$360	$237	$2,791	$49,216	$561,894	$512,678
17	83	$378,456	$49,216	$ –	$360	$254	$2,997	$52,828	$584,370	$531,543
18–19	85	$425,986	$52,828	$ –	$720	$566	$6,666	$60,779	$632,055	$571,276
20–21	87	$479,486	$60,779	$ –	$720	$650	$7,662	$69,811	$683,630	$613,819
22–23	89	$539,705	$69,811	$ –	$720	$746	$8,794	$80,071	$739,415	$659,343
24–25	91	$607,487	$80,071	$ –	$720	$856	$10,079	$91,726	$799,751	$708,025
26–27	93	$683,782	$91,726	$ –	$720	$980	$11,540	$104,965	$865,011	$760,045
28–29	95	$769,659	$104,965	$ –	$720	$1,120	$13,199	$120,004	$935,595	$815,691
30–31	97	$866,321	$120,004	$ –	$720	$1,280	$15,083	$137,088	$1,011,940	$878,852
32–33	99	$975,122	$137,088	$ –	$720	$1,462	$17,224	$156,494	$1,094,514	$938,021

Section Two
Reverse Mortgages in the Financial Plan

Reverse Mortgages, Taxes and Other Financial Products

Our primary goal in this section is to look at the uses of income streams from reverse mortgages and how they affect a client's portfolio.

Although many clients will find a reverse mortgage an attractive solution for major purchases (such as additions to homes, vacations, motor homes, boats, and other purchases of that nature), an advisor's focus will be on how monthly income can be affected and how the influx of totally tax-unencumbered funds on a monthly or periodic basis can be used to the client's advantage. The key here, of course, is the participation of a financial/insurance advisor who not only understands the basics of reverse mortgages, but also can implement strategies that will best serve clients.

When it comes to reverse mortgages the market is defined at its most basic level by those people who do and do not meet the fundamental requirements of age and equity.

For people who are at least 62 years old and have an equity position in their home, we find that they fall into one of three categories, those who need additional monthly income just to meet their basic standard or living, those who are getting by but could put the tax-free income from a reverse mortgage to good use. And those who do not need any additional income but can benefit from the tax advantages that come into play because of the tax-free funds from a reverse mortgage that will allow them to reposition other taxable assets.

The following chart illustrates how we can determine which group a person (or persons) will most likely fall into.

Figure 9.1

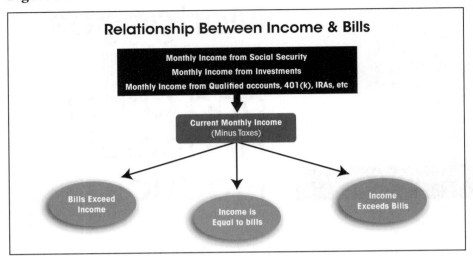

Relationship Between Income & Bills

Monthly Income from Social Security
Monthly Income from Investments
Monthly Income from Qualified accounts, 401(k), IRAs, etc

Current Monthly Income
(Minus Taxes)

Bills Exceed Income

Income is Equal to bills

Income Exceeds Bills

Many people who do not work in the retirement market come to, what appears to be, an obvious conclusion: financial planners do not have retired clients that have problems meeting their monthly income needs.

This, of course, is not the case. There are many retired people who try to establish and maintain lifestyles that exceed their incomes. Anyone that has been a planner in the retirement marketplace for any length of time will readily tell you that the consulting side of the business has a lot more to do with the psychological aspects than it does with basic number crunching. Being able to produce the desired amount of income that a client wants (as compared to the amount of income a client actually needs) is one thing, explaining financial realities and having a client understand and accept them is often something entirely different.

Understanding how reverse mortgages can be used in relation to other investment and income strategies puts an advisor in a much more advantageous position. Not only will they be able to provide their clients with options, they will also be able to provide those same clients with choices ranging from the most basic (providing increased income), to much more complex and far-reaching tax and estate planning strategies.

It is safe to say that many seniors would be better served when their financial planners not only understand, but are able to convey to them, how and why a reverse mortgage might be something they should consider. Explaining that, in fact, a reverse mortgage is nothing more than a tool that when used properly can provide positive options is essential.

So, let us take a look at not only who should consider a reverse mortgage, but why they should consider one. Prospective reverse mortgage users can look at the following chart that lists the three categories already mentioned and takes into consideration why the money might be taken from a reverse mortgage and how that additional money can affect the overall portfolio.

Figure 9.2

Who should consider a Reverse Mortgage?	
People with expenses that exceed their monthly income.	• *A reverse mortgage can provide additional tax free income to meet or exceed monthly expenses.* • *Accessing dead equity can increase income without incurring additional monthly payments.*
People with income that is equal to their expenses.	• *A reverse mortgage can provide additional tax-free income.* • *Increased income without increased taxes or required payments can provide unlimited options.*
People with income that exceeds their monthly expenses.	• *A reverse mortgage can allow other assets to be repositioned into more tax-advantaged positions.* • *By replacing taxable income with tax-free income, the overall tax bill can be reduced.*

Before we go into a much more in-depth study of each category, this would be a good time to examine what role a financial or insurance advisor should play in the reverse mortgage process. This is, of course, a matter of perception. Advisors need to decide not only what they feel about reverse mortgages but also how they think they can best serve their clients.

It is my opinion that one of the things that distinguish a poor or average advisor from a good one is the advisor's ability to understand and ensure that his prospects and clients understand certain concepts that although basic in their nature (for whatever reason) are often misunderstood.

When it comes to investing and financial and insurance planning, one of the most important concepts is the difference between perception and reality. The perception is that advice is cheap. In reality, the cost of the right financial advice is priceless (the value far exceeding the cost).

The first category is "*those people with monthly expenses that exceed their monthly income*." For some reason, many people seem to think that retirees who are not able to meet their monthly expenses are not the type to have a financial planner or advisor. Even if they did, this is not someone a good financial advisor/planner would want as a client. The reality, on the other hand, is that clients' net worth does not necessarily correspond with the amount of monthly income they generate. Likewise, the amount of income retirees' portfolios produce and the amount of money they actually spend do not necessarily coincide either. Generally, if retirees lived beyond their means while they were working, they will continue to live beyond their means after they retire. After all, there is no law that states people who have a certain amount of money necessarily know how to manage money.

Most people in the general public (and far too many in the financial/insurance industry) assume that individuals who have a hard time meeting their monthly expenses have limited or no assets. Granted, this may be the case for a great number of people who fall into the first category. It is also true that it is highly unlikely that a person with limited assets and income would, in fact, be a client of the financial/insurance advisor.

As financial/insurance advisors, we must always keep in mind that there are plenty of people with assets with significant incomes and yet they find themselves in financial straits when it comes to meeting their monthly expenses.

The client/advisor relationship can often be difficult. When it comes to addressing issues such as a reverse mortgage, the advisor may be in a very difficult position. Granted, the reverse mortgage appears to be a godsend for those whose expenses exceed their income. Unfortunately, many of the clients fail to see this new income serves as a lifeline that will help them meet their monthly needs. They may not understand that they need to follow and subscribe to a logical budget. Instead, these clients will often see these additional dollars as new disposable income and, in many cases, increase their spending habits (leaving them with even greater debt).

I know a number of advisors who have told me that a reverse mortgage *appears* to be the answer to some problems facing their clients. But the fact that these advisors cannot get their clients to restrain their spending causes great difficulty. Often, clients cannot act responsibly with the money they have, so any planner recommending a reverse mortgage rightly worries that the problem could just be exacerbated by giving such clients more expendable cash.

The second category is *"those people with income that is equal to their expenses."* This includes people living within their budget, but who have little or no room for anything outside their normal living expenses.

A reverse mortgage for these people can make a dramatic difference to their lifestyle. For one thing, if they are using all of their assets to produce the income they need to live on, there is nothing in place in the form of a growth or savings plan that can provide them with any kind of monetary cushion in case of a cash emergency. It is also important to have a financial vehicle that can maintain pace with inflation. Although there may never be a cash emergency, the effects of inflation on their overall portfolio will be detrimental over time. In these cases, the additional funds that could be provided by a reverse mortgage will allow them some leeway. This will provide them with the opportunity to build a savings account or to even put the excess funds they now have into a systematic investment vehicle.

One of the more interesting things I have seen in the past couple years is that more and more seniors are finding it harder and harder to find the money needed to make their insurance premiums for such things as their auto, homeowners, health insurance, and even long-term care premiums. In one case, the couple established a line of credit through a reverse mortgage to meet these premiums as they came due. The result was an excess of $700 per month. The plan was (and to the best my knowledge still is) to put the $700 into savings, until they had $5,000. At which time, they would start investing that $700 every month into a mutual fund. They also decided that once a year they wanted to do a little traveling. They budgeted $2,000 a year for these vacations. This, of course, would come out of the savings (which they would replenish over time with the growth they anticipated in their mutual funds).

It is important to realize that they took the money from the reverse mortgage in the form of a line of credit because it would allow them access to different amounts of money at any given time. Another thing it could provide to them was the ability to take advantage of special deals on cruises and other vacations. Whether or not you agree with the validity of using a reverse mortgage, the fact of the matter is plain to see: something as simple as establishing a line credit by way of a reverse mortgage did dramatically change this retired couple's outlook.

When it comes to these first two categories--those people who need reverse mortgages just to meet their monthly expenses and those people who are meeting their monthly income needs but would have a dramatic change in their lifestyles if they tapped into their equity via a reverse mortgage—this new source of income is dramatic. It is interesting that only a minimal amount of monthly income is needed to make these profound changes for the people in both of these lifestyle categories. But, in both of these cases, it is entirely likely that the use the funds from a reverse mortgage will not make any dramatic difference in their portfolios. True, their descendents will most likely end up with less inheritance because of the equity taken out of their homes, but these funds we are talking about is *their* money and no one should feel entitled to inherit based on unnecessary sacrifices by retired parents.

What makes reverse mortgages so inviting for people in the first two categories is the relationship between assets and income. Even though their home is (*in most cases*) their largest single asset, when it comes to retirement, it is their poorest income producer. Actually it cannot be considered a poor producer as it is not under performing compared to their other assets; it simply is not producing income at all and, as such, it should be considered what it is—dead equity.

It is hard for me to understand why so many people struggle and live with financial worries when a readily available and perfectly acceptable solution is within their reach.

A good visual illustration of this can be seen in the following chart based on information found in the "65+ in the United States, 2005" report, issued by the Department of Health and Human Service.

Figure 9.3

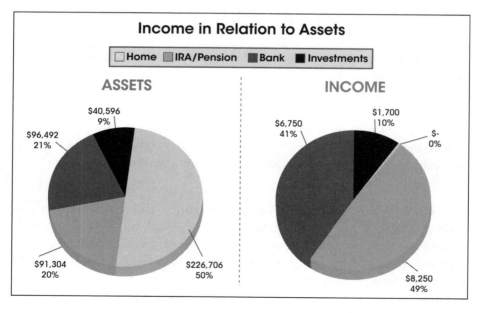

As you can see in this illustration, even though the home represents 50% of this couple's total assets, it provides nothing in the way of income. Why a retired individual or couple would struggle financially (and put up with the psychological pain in doing so when they may not have to) is beyond me.

Perhaps people do not use reverse mortgages because they do not know this option is available, or they do not understand how it works. Should either of those be the case, they would certainly benefit from their financial/insurance advisor taking a few minutes to explain the relationship between assets and income as seen in the following chart.

Figure 9.4

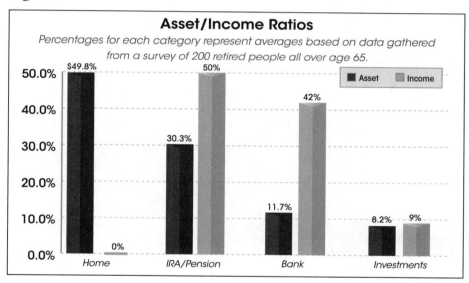

Using a Reverse Mortgage as a Tool to Reduce Income Tax

CHAPTER 10

Unlike a rose is a rose, income—at least in the eyes of the IRS—is not all the same. The IRS uses different classifications for both the kind of income received and the way in which any particular income will be taxed.

The following will take only federal income tax into consideration and nothing read in this book should be misconstrued for actual tax advice. When it comes to tax questions from a client or prospect, I strongly suggest you seek the advice of a tax professional such as a practicing CPA or tax attorney.

I fully understand that anyone reading this book more than likely does not need a refresher course on basic income taxation, and the following is not an attempt to do anything more than give you a chance to think about these things from a layman's point of view. Keep in mind that although tax-free cash from a reverse mortgage should play a large role in the decision-making process for anyone considering a reverse mortgage, my research has indicated that taxes are rarely considered in this process.

Generally speaking, we can break income down into several different kinds:

> **Earned Income** consists of salaries, bonuses, commissions, income generated from business operations, and up to 85% of payments received from Social Security.

> **Portfolio Income** is derived from dividends, interest, royalties, and capital gains or losses.

Passive Income covers things such as rental income and income received from limited partnerships, as well as any gains or losses generated from the sale of these investments.

Capital Gains are the profits realized upon the sale of a capital asset. In many cases, the amount of a capital gain is treated as income and subject to special capital gains tax rates.

Income could also be classified as follows.

Ordinary Income consists of income from wages, salaries, tips, commissions, bonuses, and other types of compensation from employment, interest, dividends, or net income from a sole proprietorship, partnership or LLC. Rents and royalties (after certain deductions) and gambling winnings are also treated as ordinary income. A "short term capital gain," or gain on the sale of an asset held for less than one year of the capital gains holding period, is also taxed as ordinary income.

Tax-Deferred can apply to both interest and appreciation. Unlike most investments where interest or gain is taxed annually as it is earned, deferred vehicles allow the taxes normally due on interest or gains to be postponed until some future date. The tax is generally triggered by a distribution, either in the form of a cash withdrawal or a payment to a beneficiary, or a sale of other disposition of an asset.

Tax-Exempt is income that is exempt from federal and/or state taxes. When it comes to tax exemptions, we most often think of municipal bonds. One thing to keep in mind when it comes to tax-exempt interest is that even though interest from tax-exempt investments is not counted when calculating federal tax owed, there is a line on federal tax returns where it must be reported. This is very important for people receiving Social Security. Even though no federal income tax is due, this income is used when calculating what amount of a person's Social Security benefits will be counted in a person's adjusted gross income. There are other items that have a tax-exempt status such as life insurance proceeds and health insurance benefits received because of medical expenses.

A tax exclusion ratio can sometimes be used to separate income from principal. In certain investments and contracts used to provide income, payments are made up of both interest and a principal. The return of principal is not taxed and is therefore excluded. For example, an exclusion ratio is used with annuities. Because part of the money being received by the owner is, in fact, part of the original deposit, it is excluded from tax. An exclusion ratio is used to determine what is reportable and what is not.

Tax Free. Although this term is often associated with municipal bonds, in reality, this may be only part of the picture. Municipals may be exempt from federal tax, but in many cases are still subject to state tax. On the other hand, interest earned from federally issued obligations may be exempt from state income taxes, but still subject to federal tax.

In addition, the interest earned for these government obligations is still included when calculating the taxable portion of social security benefits. As a result, the inclusion of this type of income may well result in a portion of one's government benefits being taxed. As such, it's hard to describe these vehicles as tax free.

In order for income to be considered truly tax free, it needs to be totally unencumbered from any tax as well as not be counted as income in any form; hence, not reported on a 1040, 1040A or any state income tax return.

Funds received from a reverse mortgage are truly tax free as they don't count as income; nor are they reportable. Because of this, reverse mortgages may be used to reduce taxes. If taxable income can be replaced with tax free income, it is possible to reduce overall tax due. This, in turn, provides the opportunity to maintain net income at the same level while increasing disposable income via the reduction of the overall tax bill.

If a person could reduce federal income tax due by $6,000 a year, would it increase disposable income by $6,000 per year? This isn't the same as making an additional $6,000 a year, as there is a difference between increased income and net income. For example, if a person in a 28% tax bracket increases annual income by $6,000, net disposable income only increases $4,320, as $1,680 is owed in additional income tax. If, on the other hand, net income doesn't change while the overall tax bill is reduced by $6,000, the entire $6,000 is available as new disposable income. Now, this doesn't mean that the person has to spend this additional $500 per month, the person might save it or pay off debt; it really doesn't matter. What does matter, especially to a retired person, is that the monthly income can be increased and the person can do this by simply taking advantage of current tax law. This is where a reverse mortgage comes into play, for not only those in the lower income brackets, but also those in the highest income brackets. Using tax free income from a reverse mortgage in conjunction with tax-deferred vehicles can make a very big difference for most seniors.

So how important is this?

Let's take a look at Median Household Income for Americans 65 years old and older in Figure 10.1.

Figure 10.1. How the median income for people over the age of 65 changes over time.

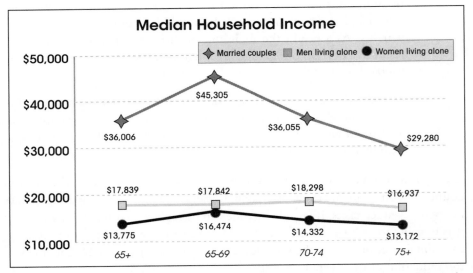

Source: U.S. Department of Health and Human Services and U.S. Department of Commerce, "65+ in the United States: 2005"

The two most troubling things about this chart is (1) the disparity of income between men and women who live alone compared to couples; and (2) that after 70, income declines. There are many reasons why couples have a greater household income than single people, but the primary reason for the decline in income for both groups after the age of 70 is that people start tapping into their principle for income. This is understandable with qualified money, as the IRS distribution requirements increase the longer a person lives. The worrisome thing is that the same erosion is seen in their nonqualified saving. Although there are numerous reasons for this principle erosion, the fundamental problem appears to be that the income they have been able to produce off their investments fails to keep pace with their income needs.

"Outliving your money" is a phrase heard on TV and from investment and insurance advisors all the time. Truth is, for a person working and years away from retirement, this might not seem like a big deal; but for a person watching his or her assets shrink, it is not only a big deal, it is scary and causes way too many sleepless nights. Many seniors would sleep better if they understood how to produce tax free income from their largest single asset.

To compound this problem, the median household net worth for seniors, which initially goes up, starts to trend downward the older the person gets. Figure 10.2 provides a good picture of an even more disturbing reality; after an initial increase in both income and net worth followed by a sharp decline, the percentage of net worth represented by the equity in their homes continues to increase.

Here's a question worth pondering. *If income and net worth reach a high point and then start to decline over time, while the percentage of net worth represented by the equity a senior has in their home continues to grow over that same period of time, why doesn't every senior who owns their home at least look at a reverse mortgage?*

Figure 10.2. The relationship between equity built up in a senior's home and the percentage that equity represents of the senior's overall net worth.

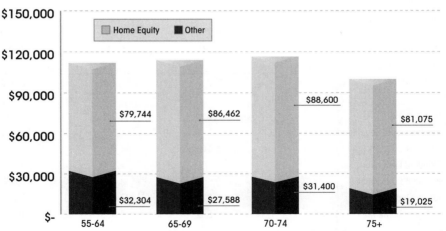

Source: U.S. Department of Health and Human Services and U.S. Department of Commerce, "65+ in the United States: 2005"

A question seniors should be asking and that a planner/advisor should be able to answer is whether or not tax free funds generated by a reverse mortgage would make a difference when it comes to their taxes. After all, doing a reverse mortgage for additional income is one thing, but increasing one's income while lowering tax is something else altogether. In order to do this, one needs to start by making sure that a client has at least a general understanding of current tax brackets and exemptions.

Figures 10.3 to 10.5 illustrate how using a reverse mortgage might change disposable income. Depending on the client's situation, reverse mortgage payments can be spent or invested. The client may also be able to reconfigure other assets because of the increased income resulting from the reverse mortgage payments.

Figure 10.3 shows three different people, all of whom are filing their income tax as single. Assumptions are based on three different sources of income: Social Security, income from qualified plan accounts, and other taxable income. In

Figure 10.3. How taxes affect net income from different taxable sources

	Client A	Client B	Client C
Year	2009	2009	2009
Taxpayer Filing	Single Return	Single Return	Single Return
Social Security	10,800	18,000	24,000
Reverse Mortgage	0	0	0
Retirement Plans	8,250	16,500	24,750
Other Taxable Income	8,315	16,565	24,880
Tax-Exempt Interest	0	0	0
Total Income	27,365	51,065	73,630
Tentative AGI	16,565	33,065	49,630
Taxable Social Security	0	11,355	20,400
Adjusted Gross Income	16,565	44,420	70,030
Standard Deductions	7,100	7,100	7,100
Personal Exemptions	3,650	3,650	3,650
Taxable Income	5,815	33,670	59,280
Federal Income Tax	582	4,633	11,008
Total Income	27,365	51,065	73,630
Federal Income Tax	582	4,633	11,008
Net Income	26,784	46,432	62,623

an effort to keep from making this unnecessarily complex, tax-exempt interest (e.g., municipal bonds or municipal bond mutual funds), capital gains, and other specially taxed property, such as annuities with tax deferral and a tax exclusion, have not been included. Retirement plan income and other taxable income are assumed to be fully taxable as ordinary income. The taxpayers use the standard deduction, including the increased deduction for those age 65 and older.

There are numerous other sources of income that can be found. It is suggested that a model be used similar to this one, adjusted to make allowances for all sources of income to accommodate each client individually. The idea here isn't to convince the client that a reverse mortgage is good or bad, but rather to show the client the numbers, so the client can make the best decision possible for the client.

On the surface, one might assume that none of these people would be in a serious tax bind, but they may well fall into one of the aforementioned categories: those not meeting their monthly income needs or those who are meeting their income needs but don't have money left over for extras or savings. If any of these clients were to add in reverse mortgage payments without any other changes, the categories of reverse mortgage, total income, and net income would be increased by the amount of the annual reverse mortgage payments.

Some clients may use the addition of reverse mortgage payments to reconfigure their other investments. Figure 10.4 illustrates what happens if a client takes out a reverse mortgage that replaces part of the other taxable income and moves that part of the money producing taxable income into a tax deferred or nontaxable vehicle, such as a deferred annuity, gold, or a stock that doesn't pay a dividend.

Client A gets an extra $525 a year. On a monthly basis, client A gets an extra $43.75 a month. This isn't much, but to a person on a low fixed income, $43.75 can make a difference.

Client B will get an extra $2,786 a year, or $232.17 a month. Client C will receive an additional $5,388 a year, or $449 a month. How this money is used and how it might affect these people will depend greatly on the individual situations they find themselves in.

The bottom line is that this new source of tax free income is replacing income they had been paying taxes on. Given the choice, regardless of the amount, many would prefer to keep that money rather than give it to the IRS.

Figure 10.4. Part of the other taxable income is replaced with tax free income from a reverse mortgage. In addition, that part of the other taxable income is changed into a tax-deferred position such as an annuity, life insurance policy, non-dividend paying stock, gold etc.

	Client A	Client B	Client C
Year	2009	2009	2009
Taxpayer Filing	Single Return	Single Return	Single Return
Social Security	10,800	18,000	24,000
Reverse Mortgage	5,250	10,500	15,750
Retirement Plans	8,250	16,500	24,750
Other Taxable Income	3,065	6,065	9,130
Tax-Exempt Interest	0	0	0
Total Income	27,365	51,065	73,630
Tentative AGI	11,315	22,565	33,880
Taxable Social Security	0	3,283	14,598
Adjusted Gross Income	11,315	25,848	48,478
Standard Deductions	7,100	7,100	7,100
Personal Exemptions	3,650	3,650	3,650
Taxable Income	565	15,098	37,728
Federal Income Tax	57	1,847	5,620
Total Income	27,365	51,065	73,630
Federal Income Tax	57	1,847	5,620
Net Income	27,309	49,218	68,011

If they had enough equity in their homes to replace all of the other taxable income, their tax savings would grow even more as can be seen in Figure 10.5.

As can be seen above, by replacing taxable income with tax free income from a reverse mortgage, the overall taxes paid goes down (as would be expected), but a more interesting event takes place when we take into consideration that by lowering the reportable income, we reduce the amount being used to calculate taxes on social security, which, in some cases, will result in an even greater reduction in tax due. People filing single returns start including social security benefits in adjusted gross income when their modified adjusted gross income plus one-half of tax-exempt interest exceeds $25,000. That number for married couples filing jointly is $32,000. As much as 85% of social security

Figure 10.5. Illustrates the changes in income and change in effective tax rate when all of the other taxable income is replaced with tax free income from a reverse mortgage. In order to achieve these numbers, the present taxable investments must be moved into tax-deferred vehicles.

	Client A	Client B	Client C
Year	2009	2009	2009
Taxpayer Filing	Single Return	Single Return	Single Return
Social Security	10,800	18,000	24,000
Reverse Mortgage	8,315	16,565	24,880
Retirement Plans	8,250	16,500	24,750
Other Taxable Income	0	0	0
Tax-Exempt Interest	0	0	0
Total Income	27,365	51,065	73,630
Tentative AGI	8,250	16,500	24,750
Taxable Social Security	0	250	6,838
Adjusted Gross Income	8,250	16,750	31,588
Standard Deductions	7,100	7,100	7,100
Personal Exemptions	3,650	3,650	3,650
Taxable Income	0	6,000	20,838
Tax	0	600	2,708
Total Income	27,365	51,065	73,630
Federal Income Tax	0	600	2,708
Net Income	27,365	50,465	70,922

benefits could be subject to tax. Because the payment received from a reverse mortgage is not included in income (it is simply a borrowed amount), it doesn't count when the formula is used to determine if social security benefits will be taxable.

From a client's perspective, it would be useful to see how the different scenarios above compare. Figures 10.6 to 10.8 show how as the reverse mortgage (RM) payments increase and a corresponding amount of otherwise taxable income is deferred, federal income tax is reduced and net income (NI) increases.

Figure 10.6 compares the three reverse mortgage scenarios above for Client A. As the reverse mortgage payments increase, federal income tax is reduced and net income increases. An amount of otherwise taxable income equal to the reverse mortgage payment is deferred in Scenarios 2 and 3.

Figure 10.6. Comparison of Reverse Mortgage Increase for Client A

Client A		Scenario	
	1	2	3
Reverse Mortgage	0	5,250	8,315
Federal Income Tax	582	57	0
Net Income	26,784	27,309	27,365
Increase		525	581

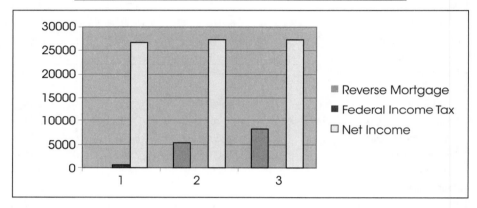

Figure 10.7 compares the three reverse mortgage scenarios above for Client B. As the reverse mortgage payments increase, federal income tax is reduced and net income increases. An amount of otherwise taxable income equal to the reverse mortgage payment is deferred in Scenarios 2 and 3.

Figure 10.8 compares the three reverse mortgage scenarios above for Client C. As the reverse mortgage payments increase, federal income tax is reduced and net income increases. An amount of otherwise taxable income equal to the reverse mortgage payment is deferred in Scenarios 2 and 3.

What is important to remember here is that replacing taxable income with tax free income generated from a reverse mortgage will by itself not reduce taxes. What is required is to shift those assets presently producing taxable income into tax-deferred positions.

The concepts in this chapter and any of its charts, graphs, and tables are not intended to be used as in whole or in part as a client presentation. They do present some ideas as to how tax free income from a reverse mortgage can change different aspects of a senior's portfolio.

Figure 10.7. Comparison of Reverse Mortgage Increase for Client B

Client B		Scenario	
	1	2	3
Reverse Mortgage	0	10,500	16,565
Federal Income Tax	4,633	1,847	600
Net Income	46,432	49,218	50,465
Increase		2,786	4,033

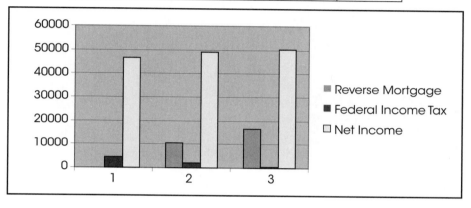

Figure 10.8. Comparison of Reverse Mortgage Increase for Client C

Client C		Scenario	
	1	2	3
Reverse Mortgage	0	15,750	24,880
Federal Income Tax	11,008	5,620	2,708
Net Income	62,623	68,011	70,922
Increase		5,388	8,299

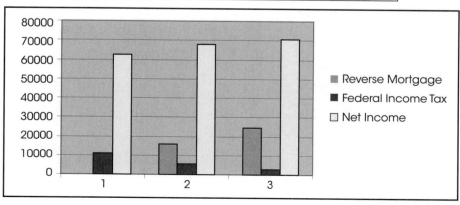

Value and Net Appreciation

One thing kept coming up again and again while doing the research and writing of this book. Not only are most people totally unfamiliar with how reverse mortgages work, most of those who do think they understand reverse mortgages and have drawn conclusions as to their value have based those conclusions on misconceptions. When I started doing research for this book, it quickly became apparent that even I was under a totally different impression. As I did more and more research, it became obvious to me that my previous opinion was incorrect and was reached on erroneous perceptions rather than based on facts.

When it comes to reverse mortgages, far too many people allow themselves to form opinions based on the ill-conceived notion that perception is reality; when in fact perception is nothing more than an individual person's point of view, which may or may not make any distinctions between fact and fantasy.

This chapter will attempt to clear up some of these misconceptions and/or change the perspective; thus, giving people a reason to look or relook at reverse mortgages from a better-educated point of view and with a more open mind.

First, I want to address the concepts of equity, net gain, and net appreciation. While doing research for this book, I spoke to a number of people about the equity they had in their homes. Most of the people I spoke to that had a mortgage on their property responded that their equity was the difference between the market value of their home and the amount of money needed to pay off their mortgage. When I spoke to people who owned their homes outright (free of any mortgage), they stated that their equity was the market value of their home. Herein lies the rub: when looking at a reverse mortgage, the equity of the property is one thing. But what needs to be taken into consideration and what many people often overlook is the true cost of owning a home. I prefer to look at the net gain and determine net appreciation.

When borrowers receive tax-free money from a reverse mortgage, I suggest three connected but different things must be taken into consideration—the initial sales price of the property, the amount of interest paid during the life of the mortgage, and the amount of money saved in taxes because of the write-off the IRS allows on interest paid on mortgages. Looking at those three items results in net appreciation. When I say "net appreciation," what I mean is the true net gain in a home after all costs, which includes the downpayment and principal and after-tax interest payments.

In an effort to provide more clarity on this concept, I have put together Figure 11.1 to help provide a visual interpretation. The numbers used in Figure 11.1 come from an actual reverse mortgage case. The appraised value, the original purchase price, and the amount of interest paid over the life of the mortgage are real-life numbers. But, in reference to the changes in their income and tax brackets over the life of the mortgage, the clients could not provide me with the actual dollar amount saved through tax write-offs. As such, the assumption used in Figure 11.1 for the dollar amount saved from the tax deduction the IRS allows on mortgage interest uses the 28% tax rate (which in all likelihood would not be the actual case and is only being used here for illustration purposes). Figure 11.1 is not intended to provide an absolutely accurate picture, but rather a fairly good view of the different components making up this illustration.

As you can see from Figure 11.1, the original purchase price of the home was $47,152 and a 30-year mortgage was used to buy this home. Over that 30-year period, $106,603 was paid in interest of which *(because of the deductibility of interest allowed by the IRS)* this couple saved $29,849 in taxes. As to what they did with that $29,849, I have no idea. It may have been used to pay down debt, invested, or they may have spent it in any number of ways. It really does not matter. What does matter is that because of a write off, they reduced their taxes owed by $29,849 which, in effect, increased their disposable income by that same amount.

Figure 11.1

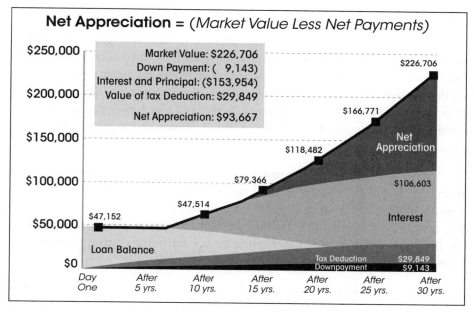

Based on these numbers we can draw the following conclusions:

(1) From the time they bought their home until the time they wrote a reverse mortgage on that home, the value had grown from $47,152 to $226,706, which is an increase of $179,554.

(2) When they did the reverse mortgage, the amount they had paid into the mortgage in principal and interest (plus the downpayment) was $162,888. However, we must take into consideration that because their interest was deductible over those 30 years, their disposable income increased by $29,849. This means that the net amount they had paid into the mortgage in principal and interest (plus the downpayment) was $133,039.

(3) When they did the reverse mortgage, the difference between the appraised value and the amount they had paid into the mortgage in principal and interest (plus the downpayment) was $63,818. However, we must take into consideration that because their interest was deductible over those 30 years, their disposable income increased by $29,849. This means that the true difference between the appraised value and the net amount they paid into the mortgage in principal and interest (plus the downpayment) was $93,667.

So why do I think this concept is so important? Because of the following...

When borrowers receive money from a reverse mortgage, the money comes to them totally tax unencumbered. What I mean by that is that, unlike tax-exempt interest *(which they do not pay federal income tax on but do have to report on their annual tax return and which also counts against them when doing their Social Security tax calculations)*, or tax-deferred *gains (which they have to pay income tax on when they are withdrawn)*, funds received from a reverse mortgage are not taxable or reported.

Now let's take a look at that first $93,000 they withdrew via a reverse mortgage. Is it in reality gain? The answer to that question has to be yes. It is my version of "net appreciation." And, even better, they will not be required to pay any tax on this gain. This means that their money has grown, tax-deferred, for 30 years and is now being withdrawn tax free. (Of course, gain may be taxed later when the house is sold.)

Another thing to ponder is why so many people think that, when individuals do a reverse mortgage, they are only getting their own principal back. It appears that these people fail to take into consideration that not only is 41% of the appraised value of their home in fact pure gain, they are also able to get tax free that portion of the interest that they wrote off over the years their original mortgage was in place.

Asset and Liability

Now that we have looked at net gain *(aka net appreciation)*, let's take a different look at a home and its unique status as both an asset and a liability. The reason we look at this when dealing with reverse mortgages is because, contrary to popular opinion, neither the asset nor the liability aspects of home ownership change very much.

A good exercise to do for yourself, and certainly to do with your clients, would be to sit down and use the old Benjamin Franklin decision making process. Take a piece of paper, draw a line down the middle, and on the left side list all the advantages or assets to home ownership. On the right side lists all the disadvantages or liabilities. I find it interesting that when I do this with someone, even though the things on their list are almost always the same, what they consider assets and liabilities varies greatly from person to person. Another thing you might notice when you do this list is how many people list things as either an asset or liability that have nothing to do with the home.

In Figure 11.2, I have listed what I consider the four most important things to consider when considering whether or not a person should do a reverse mortgage. Keep in mind that this short and straight to the point list will almost certainly be similar to one you or your clients might put together.

Figure 11.2

Home Ownership	
Asset	**Liability**
Equity	Depreciation
Appreciation	Maintenance
Possible Income Stream	Insurance
Tax Write Offs	Taxes

Of course, equity is the primary asset. However, when I started writing this book, I never gave any consideration that home ownership could also be considered the source of an unencumbered income stream. As for the liabilities, like everyone else, my property is at risk of losing value through depreciation, something that few people thought possible until this last downturn in the real estate market. Now everyone knows that real estate, like any other investment, can go down as well as up. I consider insurance payments as a liability even though I wouldn't be foolish enough not to have insurance and take the risk of assuming that true liability on my own. And last, but not least, I consider the taxes as a liability. If at some future date I was to do a reverse mortgage, I don't think my list would change much, if at all. Most likely, the only thing that would be different is where I would list the tax write-offs.

On the liability side, I would stay wary of depreciation. However, one of the benefits of using a reverse mortgage is that, regardless of whether or not my house depreciates in value, the amount of my reverse mortgage can't be called or reconfigured to reflect a new dollar amount. If, on the other hand, my house did appreciate, it might be possible to increase the amount of my reverse mortgage loan.

When it comes to taxes and maintenance, there is no difference in whether or not a reverse mortgage is in place. As such, when taking into consideration the assets and liabilities that home ownership represents, we should keep in mind that for those items a reverse mortgage doesn't really change anything.

Cost

One of the biggest points of contention for people who are negative about reverse mortgages is the costs related to creating and putting in force a reverse mortgage. Using math and variable statistics, I can easily come up with 10 different scenarios that will prove or disprove this perception. Perhaps a better question would be how expensive a reverse mortgage is, as opposed to some alternative.

Because a person has to be least 62 years old to even do a reverse mortgage, it is safe to assume that we're normally talking about seniors who will soon, if not already, be retired. In my opinion, it makes a difference in the reverse mortgage decision process whether or not a person is still working and, if the person is still working, how much longer the person intends to work. When considering cost, we shouldn't limit the issue to the reverse mortgage, but should also take into account what, if any, alternatives are available that would meet the needs or desires of these people that are less expensive than a reverse mortgage.

If the goal is to generate income, and a substantial portion of one's portfolio is represented by an asset that is thoroughly underperforming (*from an income producing point of view*), the cost of converting that asset into an income producing vehicle is only relevant if we compare the transaction to the cost of another transaction that will produce an equal or greater amount of income.

In order to do that with a home, our options are limited.

(1) You can sell the home, put the sales proceeds into an interest-bearing investment, and live off the additional income. This, of course, leaves you with a small problem of not having a place to live, which can be solved by buying another home, renting a place, or moving in with someone else. Most people would find any of those three less than desirable, but they are options.

(2) A second option would be to take out a home equity loan or to establish a new mortgage on the property. Both of these have costs associated with setting them up. More importantly, both require

ongoing payments and can significantly reduce the overall equity of the home.

(3) The third option is to do a reverse mortgage, which does have costs associated with its establishment. What most people don't know (*and, as a financial advisor, you need to be aware of*) is that those costs are negotiable. Far too often when talking about reverse mortgages, I hear people say that the only place they can go to get one is the FHA. In reality, there is another option, using a private mortgage company that is not backed by the FHA.

Of course, you need to use due diligence and make sure the company you are dealing with is an established professional organization and make sure that all benefits you enjoy from an FHA loan are incorporated in the private company's documentation.

Figure 11.3 shows how a person was able to increase monthly income by taking a reverse mortgage and shifting a lump sum of money from a certificate of deposit into a tax–deferred annuity. In this case, although the amount they received monthly stayed the same, the amount they had to spend actually increased because they were able to replace taxable income with totally tax–free income.

Figure 11.3

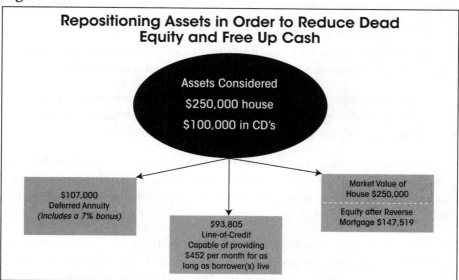

- 93 -

If you look at this illustration closely, you may come to the conclusion that the cost of establishing that line of credit to the reverse mortgage came to $8,676 ($250,000 – $147,519 – $93,805). Now, look at that as a percentage of the overall value of the property; it represents 3.47%. If, on the other hand, you look at that same amount as a percentage of the $93,805 line of credit, it represents 9.25%.

Is that expensive? Yes. But we need to put this into a more general perspective. Had they sold their home outright at $250,000, *and* were able to get a mortgage broker to sell that house for 5.5%, they would've paid $13,750 to the broker. And let's not forget, they would then be in need of a place to live, which would require either another real-estate commission, if they buy another place, or ongoing rent payments.

If they took out an equity loan, what they end up paying is an untold amount. We have to take into consideration the cost involved in setting up the loan, as well as the interest and principal payments required to keep the loan in force. For example, if they took out a home equity loan for $50,000 at 7% and paid it back over five years, they would incur an additional monthly expense of $990.06 and, over the period of the loan, pay back $59,404.

Assuming that you can get a home equity loan at 7% and that the rate doesn't increase during the duration of the loan, they would be incurring additional expenses of $9,404 ($59,404 – $50,000), which doesn't included the cost they would incur in the generation of the equity loan.

In addition, we should remember that most people looking at a reverse mortgage aren't interested in taking on any additional monthly expenses.

For those people who are barely meeting their income needs, cost is, for the most part, irrelevant. Cost plays little or no part in addressing the paramount issue they face, which is having enough money to live on.

For everyone else, it is a factor that should be taken into consideration. It should also be taken into consideration that the costs related to a reverse mortgage are not set in stone, but rather are negotiable; as such, they should be shopped.

If we sit back and look at all the alternatives available to seniors, it seems a little silly that there are people out there automatically eliminating reverse mortgages because of perceived notions. It would be just as silly for someone to recommend to a client a reverse mortgage without investigating the other options available to them.

The bottom line is this: a reverse mortgage is nothing more than a tool that may or may not be able to help you, or your clients, meet their needs or desires. As everyone who has ever worked on a car or a small home repair, or even worked in his or her garden, knows, having the right tool for the job makes all the difference.

Value

So, what is the value of a reverse mortgage? I can honestly say, I don't know.

What I do know is that, when it comes to reverse mortgages, I can't find a definition in the dictionary that seems to fit. On the other hand, I can do calculations and make comparisons with different alternatives that allow me to make a good conscience recommendation based on an individual circumstance. After all, in two totally different circumstances, I recommended one to my mother-in-law and against doing one for a friend. In both cases, I felt my suggestion was made as a professional and based on overwhelming evidence.

In short, it's not a one size fits all product. It is a tool that, when used properly, can be quite advantageous.

CHAPTER 12

In Conclusion

It doesn't really matter how we, as insurance planners or financial planners or advisors, feel about reverse mortgages. Like them or not, there are a lot more reasons to believe that reverse mortgages will continue to grow in popularity than there are that they will decrease.

The above comment is based on is the following facts.

In order to qualify for a reverse mortgage, the home owner or owners have to be at least 62 years old and have equity in their home. Now combine that with these two words: "baby boomers." This represents a huge market that will continue to grow for the next 20 years or more.

Boomers are those 78 million Americans born between 1946 and 1964 who now make up somewhere around 26% of our population. The Social Security Administration projects that in 2031 there will be 57.8 million baby boomers still with us between the ages of 66 and 84, of which 55% will be women. Now combine that with another projection, that there will only be 2.1 workers for each Social Security beneficiary, as compared to today when we have 3.3 workers for each Social Security beneficiary.

Based on numerous surveys, we have concluded that only 34% of boomers think they will have enough money to live comfortably after they retire, 40% are not sure whether or not they will have enough money to live comfortably, and the remaining 29% are seriously concerned about having enough money to live on, let alone to live comfortably. Aside from those statistics, it appears that one-fourth of Boomers do not think they will have enough money to retire and will continue to work indefinitely. Also, the ever increasing cost of health care for seniors is critical. According to the Bureau of Labor Statistics, "when budgeting medical expenses, baby boomers should expect increased health-care spending as they age." For instance, in 2004, those ages 55 to 64 spent $3,262 and those 65 and over, $3,899. When adjusted for inflation in the health care industry, those numbers become as follows: $4,163 for those ages 55 to 64 and $4,976 for those 65 and over, or 19.5% more for that same health care.

Now think about the following for a minute.

There are more Americans over 62 years old today than there were yesterday, and there are going to be more people over 62 years old tomorrow than there are today, and that is going to be true for many years to come.

Due to the growth in those receiving social security benefits and the decline in the number of people paying into the social security system, the federal government will not be able to increase benefits for retirees in the future, and in all likelihood the federal government will have to decrease benefits.

As the number of people over 65 continues to increase, the cost of health care for that group will also continue to increase.

For the average American over 65 years old, their home represents 49.6% of their total net worth and it isn't producing any income.

Although opinions may differ as to the need for or the advantage of using a reverse mortgage, it is very hard to deny that the evidence is overwhelming and the use of this product will continue to grow. This leaves only one question for planners and advisors to address: Are they going to learn what they need to know about reverse mortgage in order to provide their clients with advice about how using a reverse mortgage will affect their portfolio, or ignore this area all together?

The Brave New World

Due to recent economic conditions, how we address the needs for income and growth for our clients has changed dramatically, and there is no reason to believe that it will ever be the same again. When it comes to retired people and seniors, a different scenario must be addressed; the older a person is, the less likely it is that the person will have the time it will take to recover from any loss of principal. Combine that with the need to maintain a level of income that they may not be able to do without invading a now lower principal base and we find that many older Americans now find themselves in very uncomfortable, precarious positions. They can either cut their income or start further reducing their principal base by withdrawing the additional income from their base investments.

Although they may never have considered a reverse mortgage in the past, reexamining the possibility of drawing on the thousands of dollars locked up in the equity of their homes that here-to-fore were never going to be realized by them (but rather their heirs), it may well be time to consider the options that a reverse mortgage can provide.

Appendices

APPENDIX A

Federal Regulation Z

Subpart E—Special Rules for Certain Home Mortgage Transactions
226.33 Requirements for Reverse Mortgages.

(a) _Definition_. For purposes of this subpart, _reverse mortgage transaction_ means a nonrecourse consumer credit obligation in which: (1) A mortgage, deed of trust, or equivalent consensual security interest securing one or more advances is created in the consumer's principal dwelling; and (2) Any principal, interest, or shared appreciation or equity is due and payable (other than in the case of default) only after:

    (i)   The consumer dies;

    (ii) The dwelling is transferred; or

    (iii) The consumer ceases to occupy the dwelling as a principal dwelling.

(b) _Content of disclosures_. In addition to other disclosures required by this part, in a reverse mortgage transaction the creditor shall provide the following disclosures in a form substantially similar to the model form found in paragraph (d) of Appendix K of this part:

    (1) _Notice_. A statement that the consumer is not obligated to complete the reverse mortgage transaction merely because the consumer has received the disclosures required by this section or has signed an application for a reverse mortgage loan.

(2) *Total annual loan cost rates.* A good–faith projection of the total cost of the credit determined in accordance with paragraph (c) of this section and expressed as a table of "total annual loan cost rates," using that term, in accordance with Appendix K of this part.

(3) *Itemization of pertinent information.* An itemization of loan terms, charges, the age of the youngest borrower and the appraised property value.

(4) *Explanation of table.* An explanation of the table of total annual loan cost rates as provided in the model form found in paragraph (d) of Appendix K of this part.

(c) **Projected total cost of credit.** The projected total cost of credit shall reflect the following factors, as applicable:

(1) *Costs to consumer.* All costs and charges to the consumer, including the costs of any annuity the consumer purchases as part of the reverse mortgage transaction.

(2) *Payments to consumer.* All advances to and for the benefit of the consumer, including annuity payments that the consumer will receive from an annuity that the consumer purchases as part of the reverse mortgage transaction.

(3) *Additional creditor compensation.* Any shared appreciation or equity in the dwelling that the creditor is entitled by contract to receive.

(4) *Limitations on consumer liability.* Any limitation on the consumer's liability (such as nonrecourse limits and equity conservation agreements).

(5) *Assumed annual appreciation rates.* Each of the following assumed annual appreciation rates for the dwelling: (i) 0 percent. (ii) 4 percent. (iii) 8 percent.

(6) *Assumed loan period.*

(i) Each of the following assumed loan periods, as provided in Appendix L of this part:

(A) Two years.

(B) The actuarial life expectancy of the consumer to become obligated on the reverse mortgage transaction (as of that consumer's most recent birthday). In the case of multiple consumers, the period shall be the actuarial life expectancy of the youngest consumer (as of that consumer's most recent birthday).

(C) The actuarial life expectancy specified by paragraph (c)(6)(i) (B) of this section, multiplied by a factor of 1.4 and rounded to the nearest full year.

(ii) At the creditor's option, the actuarial life expectancy specified by paragraph (c)(6)(i)(B) of this section, multiplied by a factor of .5 and rounded to the nearest full year.

Appendix K to Part 226—Total Annual Loan Cost Rate Computations for Reverse Mortgage Transactions

(a) *Introduction.* Creditors are required to disclose a series of total annual loan cost rates for each reverse mortgage transaction. This appendix contains the equations creditors must use in computing the total annual loan cost rate for various transactions, as well as instructions, explanations, and examples for various transactions. This appendix is modeled after Appendix J of this part (Annual Percentage Rates Computations for Closed-end Credit Transactions); creditors should consult Appendix J of this part for additional guidance in using the formulas for reverse mortgages.

(b) *Instructions and equations for the total annual loan cost rate*

(1) *General rule.* The total annual loan cost rate shall be the nominal total annual loan cost rate determined by multiplying the unit-period rate by the number of unit-periods in a year.

(2) *Term of the transaction.* For purposes of total annual loan cost disclosures, the term of a reverse mortgage transaction is assumed to begin on the first of the month in which consummation is expected to occur. If a loan cost or any portion of a loan cost is initially incurred beginning on a date later than consummation, the term of the transaction is assumed to begin on the first of the month in which that loan cost is incurred. For purposes of total annual loan cost disclosures, the term ends on each of the assumed loan periods specified in §226.33(c)(6).

(3) *Definitions of time intervals.*

    (i)   A *period* is the interval of time between advances.

    (ii) A *common period* is any period that occurs more than once in a transaction.

    (iii) A *standard interval of time* is a day, week, semimonth, month, or a multiple of a week or a month up to, but not exceeding, 1 year.

    (iv) All months shall be considered to have an equal number of days.

(4) *Unit-period.*

    (i)   In all transactions other than single-advance, single-payment transactions, the unit-period shall be that common period, not to exceed one year, that occurs most frequently in the transaction, except that:

    (A) If two or more common periods occur with equal frequency, the smaller of such common periods shall be the unit-period; or

    (B) If there is no common period in the transaction, the unit-period shall be that period which is the average of all periods rounded to the nearest whole standard interval of time. If the average is equally near two standard intervals of time, the lower shall be the unit-period.

    (ii) In a single-advance, single-payment transaction, the unit-period shall be the term of the transaction, but shall not exceed one year.

(5) *Number of unit-periods between two given dates.* (i) The number of days between two dates shall be the number of 24-hour intervals between any point in time on the first date to the same point in time on the second date.

    (ii) If the unit-period is a month, the number of full unit-periods between two dates shall be the number of months. If the unit-period is a month, the number of unit-periods per year shall be 12.

(iii) If the unit-period is a semimonth or a multiple of a month not exceeding 11 months, the number of days between two dates shall be 30 times the number of full months. The number of full unit-periods shall be determined by dividing the number of days by 15 in the case of a semimonthly unit-period or by the appropriate multiple of 30 in the case of a multi-monthly unit-period. If the unit-period is a semimonth, the number of unit-periods per year shall be 24. If the number of unit-periods is a multiple of a month, the number of unit-periods per year shall be 12 divided by the number of months per unit-period.

(iv) If the unit-period is a day, a week, or a multiple of a week, the number of full unit-periods shall be determined by dividing the number of days between the two given dates by the number of days per unit-period. If the unit-period is a day, the number of unit-periods per year shall be 365. If the unit-period is a week or a multiple of a week, the number of unit-periods per year shall be 52 divided by the number of weeks per unit-period.

(v) If the unit-period is a year, the number of full unit-periods between two dates shall be the number of full years (each equal to 12 months).

(6) *Symbols.* The symbols used to express the terms of a transaction in the equation set forth in paragraph (b)(8) of this appendix are defined as follows:

A_j=The amount of each periodic or lump-sum advance to the consumer under the reverse mortgage transaction.

i=Percentage rate of the total annual loan cost per unit-period, expressed as a decimal equivalent.

j=The number of unit-periods until the jth advance.

n=The number of unit-periods between consummation and repayment of the debt.

P_n=Min (Bal_n, Val_n). This is the maximum amount that the creditor can be repaid at the specified loan term.

Bal_n=Loan balance at time of repayment, including all costs and fees incurred by the consumer (including any shared appreciation or shared equity amount) compounded to time n at the creditor's contract rate of interest.

$\text{Val}_n = \text{Val}_0(1 + \sigma)^y$, where Val_0 is the property value at consummation, σ is the assumed annual rate of appreciation for the dwelling, and y is the number of years in the assumed term. Val_n must be reduced by the amount of any equity reserved for the consumer by agreement between the parties, or by 7 percent (or the amount or percentage specified in the credit agreement), if the amount required to be repaid is limited to the net proceeds of sale.

σ = The summation operator.

Symbols used in the examples shown in this appendix are defined as follows:

FV_x^i = The future value of 1 per unit period for x unit periods, first advance due immediately (at time = 0, which is consummation).

$$= \sum_{j-0}^{x-1} (1 + i)^{x-j}$$

$$= (1+ i)^x + (1+ i)^{x-1} + \cdots (1+ i)^1; \; or$$

$$= \frac{(1+ i)^n - 1}{i} \times (1+ i)$$

w = The number of unit-periods per year.

I = wi×100 = the nominal total annual loan cost rate.

(7) *General equation.* The total annual loan cost rate for a reverse mortgage transaction must be determined by first solving the following formula, which sets forth the relationship between the advances to the consumer and the amount owed to the creditor under the terms of the reverse mortgage agreement for the loan cost rate per unit-period (the loan cost rate per unit-period is then multiplied by the number of unit-periods per year to obtain the total annual loan cost rate I; that is, I = wi):

$$= \sum_{j-0}^{n-1} A_j(1 + i)^{n-j} = P_n$$

8.   *Solution of general equation by iteration process.* (i) The general equation in paragraph (b)(7) of this appendix, when applied to a simple transaction for a reverse mortgage loan of equal monthly advances of $350 each, and with a total amount owed of $14,313.08 at an assumed repayment period of two years, takes the special form:

$$P_n = 350 \ FV_{24.} \ i, \ or$$

$$P_n = 350 \ x \left[\frac{(1+ i)^n - 1}{i} \ x(1 + i) \right]$$

Using the iteration procedures found in steps 1 through 4 of (b)(9)(i) of Appendix J of this part, the total annual loan cost rate, correct to two decimals, is 48.53%.

(ii)   In using these iteration procedures, it is expected that calculators or computers will be programmed to carry all available decimals throughout the calculation and that enough iterations will be performed to make virtually certain that the total annual loan cost rate obtained, when rounded to two decimals, is correct. Total annual loan cost rates in the examples below were obtained by using a 10-digit programmable calculator and the iteration procedure described in Appendix J of this part.

(9)   *Assumption for discretionary cash advances.* If the consumer controls the timing of advances made after consummation (such as in a credit line arrangement), the creditor must use the general formula in paragraph (b)(7) of this appendix. The total annual loan cost rate shall be based on the assumption that 50 percent of the principal loan amount is advanced at closing, or in the case of an open-end transaction, at the time the consumer becomes obligated under the plan. Creditors shall assume the advances are made at the interest rate then in effect and that no further advances are made to, or repayments made by, the consumer during the term of the transaction or plan.

(10)   *Assumption for variable-rate reverse mortgage transactions.* If the interest rate for a reverse mortgage transaction may increase during the loan term and the amount or timing is not known at consummation, creditors shall base the disclosures on the initial interest rate in effect at the time the disclosures are provided.

(11) *Assumption for closing costs.* In calculating the total annual loan cost rate, creditors shall assume all closing and other consumer costs are financed by the creditor.

(c) ***Examples of total annual loan cost rate computations —***

(1) *Lump-sum advance at consummation.*

Lump-sum advance to consumer at consummation: $30,000

Total of consumer's loan costs financed at consummation: $4,500

Contract interest rate: 11.60%

Estimated time of repayment (based on life expectancy of a consumer at age 78): 10 years

Appraised value of dwelling at consummation: $100,000

Assumed annual dwelling appreciation rate: 4%

$P_{10} = Min\ (103,385.84,\ 137,662.72)$

$$30,000\ (1+i)^{10\text{-}0} + \sum_{j\text{-}0}^{9} 0(1+i)^{10\text{-}j} = 103,385.84$$

$i = .1317069438$

Total annual loan cost rate $(100(.1317069438 \times 1)) = 13.17\%$

(2) *Monthly advance beginning at consummation.*

Monthly advance to consumer, beginning at consummation: $492.51

Total of consumer's loan costs financed at consummation: $4,500

Contract interest rate: 9.00%

Estimated time of repayment (based on life expectancy of a consumer at age 78): 10 years

Appraised value of dwelling at consummation: $100,000

Assumed annual dwelling appreciation rate: 8%

$$P_{120} = Min \ (107,053.63, \ 200,780.02)$$

$$492.51 \times \left[\frac{(1+i)^{120} - 1}{i} \times (1+i) \right] = 107,053.63$$

$$i = .009061140$$

Total annual loan cost rate (100(.009061140 × 12))=10.87%

   (3) *Lump sum advance at consummation and monthly advances thereafter.*

Lump sum advance to consumer at consummation: $10,000

Monthly advance to consumer, beginning at consummation: $725

Total of consumer's loan costs financed at consummation: $4,500

Contract rate of interest: 8.5%

Estimated time of repayment (based on life expectancy of a consumer at age 75): 12 years

Appraised value of dwelling at consummation: $100,000

Assumed annual dwelling appreciation rate: 8%

$$P_{144} = Min \ (221,818.30, \ 234,189.82)$$

$$10,000 \ (1+i)^{144-0} + \sum_{j-0}^{143} 725(1+i)^{144-j} = 221,818.30$$

$$i = .007708844$$

Total annual loan cost rate (100(.007708844 × 12)) = 9.25%

(d) ***Reverse mortgage model form and sample form —(1) Model form.***

Total Annual Loan Cost Rate

Loan Terms

Age of youngest borrower:

Appraised property value:

Interest rate:

Monthly advance:

Initial draw:

Line of credit:

Initial Loan Charges

Closing costs:

Mortgage insurance premium:

Annuity cost:

Monthly Loan Charges

Servicing fee:

Other Charges:

Mortgage insurance:

Shared Appreciation:

Repayment Limits

Assumed annual appreciation	Total annual loan cost rate			
	2-year loan term	[ ]-year loan term	[ ]-year loan term	[ ]-year loan term
0%		[ ]		
4%		[ ]		
8%		[ ]		

The cost of any reverse mortgage loan depends on how long you keep the loan and how much your house appreciates in value. Generally, the longer you keep a reverse mortgage, the lower the total annual loan cost rate will be.

This table shows the estimated cost of your reverse mortgage loan, expressed as an annual rate. It illustrates the cost for three [four] loan terms: 2 years, [half of life expectancy for someone your age,] that life expectancy, and 1.4 times that life expectancy. The table also shows the cost of the loan, assuming the value of your home appreciates at three different rates: 0%, 4% and 8%.

The total annual loan cost rates in this table are based on the total charges associated with this loan. These charges typically include principal, interest, closing costs, mortgage insurance premiums, annuity costs, and servicing costs (but not costs when you sell the home).

The rates in this table are estimates. Your actual cost may differ if, for example, the amount of your loan advances varies or the interest rate on your mortgage changes.

Signing an Application or Receiving These Disclosures Does Not Require You To Complete This Loan

(2) Sample Form.

Total Annual Loan Cost Rate

Loan Terms

Age of youngest borrower: 75

Appraised property value: $100,000

Interest rate: 9%

Monthly advance: $301.80

Initial draw: $1,000

Line of credit: $4,000

Initial Loan Charges

Closing costs: $5,000

Mortgage insurance premium: None

Annuity cost: None

Monthly Loan Charges

Servicing fee: None

Other Charges

Mortgage insurance: None

Shared Appreciation: None

Repayment Limits

Net proceeds estimated at 93% of projected home sale

Assumed annual appreciation	Total annual loan cost rate			
	2-year loan term	[6-year loan term]	12-year loan term	17-year loan term
0%	39.00%	[14.94%]	9.86%	3.87%
4%	39.00%	[14.94%]	11.03%	10.14%
8%	39.00%	[14.94%]	11.03%	10.20%

The cost of any reverse mortgage loan depends on how long you keep the loan and how much your house appreciates in value. Generally, the longer you keep a reverse mortgage, the lower the total annual loan cost rate will be.

This table shows the estimated cost of your reverse mortgage loan, expressed as an annual rate. It illustrates the cost for three [four] loan terms: 2 years, [half of life expectancy for someone your age,] that life expectancy, and 1.4 times that life expectancy. The table also shows the cost of the loan, assuming the value of your home appreciates at three different rates: 0%, 4% and 8%.

The total annual loan cost rates in this table are based on the total charges associated with this loan. These charges typically include principal, interest, closing costs, mortgage insurance premiums, annuity costs, and servicing costs (but not disposition costs—costs when you sell the home).

The rates in this table are estimates. Your actual cost may differ if, for example, the amount of your loan advances varies or the interest rate on your mortgage changes.

Signing an Application or Receiving These Disclosures Does Not Require You To Complete This Loan

HUD
Handbook

Appendix 22

4235.1 REV-1 Appendix 22

HOME EQUITY CONVERSION MORTGAGE

PAYMENT CALCULATION FORMULAS

In this appendix the algebraic formulas necessary to calculate payments to borrowers are given.

1. Principal Limit:

$PL_k = PL_1 (1 + i)^{(k-1)}$ where PL_k is the principal limit in the kth month of the loan, and this principal limit is constant during the entire month,

PL_1 is the principal limit at origination and is obtained by multiplying the principal limit factor provided by the Secretary by the maximum claim amount.

(NOTE: For loans originated mid-month, the principal limit at origination is the principal limit for the first month of the loan, and is considered to have been in effect since the first day of the origination month), and is the monthly compounding rate calculated as one twelfth of the sum of the expected average mortgage rate and the annual MIP rate (0.5 percent). For example, if the expected average mortgage rate is 10 percent, then $i = (0.10 + 0.005)/12 = 0.00875$. The compounding rate does not change during the life of the loan. NOTE: The principal limit is not subject to per diem compounding when mid-month computations are made.

2. Servicing Fee Set Aside:

$S\{Sub\ k\} = FEE \times [(1+i)\{Sup(m+1)\} - (1+i)] / [i \times (1+i)\{Sup\ m\}]$, where $S\{Sub\ k\}$ is the set aside of principal limit required in the kth month of the loan for future payment of flat monthly loan servicing fees from the borrower's account, and this amount is constant for the entire month, minus the number of remaining months that the servicing fee could be collected, i.e., the remaining term on a tenure mortgage in the kth month of the loan: $m = 12 \times (100 - Borrower's\ Initial\ Age) - k + 1$, and FEE is the monthly loan servicing fee charged to the borrower's account.

NOTE: If loan servicing charges are included in the interest rate and thereby paid as a percentage of the outstanding loan balance, then FEE is zero, and the calculation of $S\{Sub\ k\}$ results in a zero set aside amount for all months. In all other cases, the servicing set aside, $S\{Sub\ k\}$, decreases as k increases, reaching zero for $k = 12\times(100-Age)$.

3. Net Principal Limit:

$NPL\{Sub\ k\} = max\ [\ 0,\ PL\{Sub\ k\} - S\{Sub\ k\} - B\{Sub\ k\}\ ]$, where $NPL\ \{Sub\ k\}$ is the net principal limit in the kth month of the loan, $PL\{Sub\ k\}$ is the principal limit in the kth month from equation (1), $S\{Sub\ k\}$ is the servicing set aside of principal limit from equation (2), and $B\{Sub\ k\}$ is the total loan balance in the kth month, including payments to or on behalf of the borrower (whether scheduled or unscheduled), interest at the note rate, and MIP.

NOTE: B is subject to per diem interest and MIP for mid-month calculation. At origination, i.e., $k = 1$, the balance is the initial loan balance.

4. Principal Limit for Line of Credit: $LOC\{Sub\ k\} = LOC\{Sub\ 1\}\ (1 + i)\{Sup\ (k-1)\}$, where $LOC\{Sub\ k\}$ is the principal limit for the line of credit in the kth month of the loan, and this principal limit is constant for the entire month (no per diem compounding for mid-month calculations), and $LOC\{Sub\ 1\}$ is the principal limit established for the line of credit at origination, and must not exceed $NPL\ \{Sub\ 1\}$ from equation (3). (NOTE: $LOC\{Sub\ 1\}$ must be large enough to cover required set asides for repairs after closing and first year taxes and insurance, if any.)

5. Available Line of Credit: $ALC\{Sub\ k\} = \max [\ 0, LOC\{Sub\ k\} - D\{Sub\ k\} - R - T\ ]$, where $ALC\{Sub\ k\}$ is the available line of credit in the kth month of the loan, $LOC\{Sub\ k\}$ is the principal limit of the line of credit from equation (4), $D\{Sub\ k\}$ is the portion of the loan balance attributable to the line of credit in the kth month (i.e., the sum of all drawdowns on the line of credit since origination plus interest at the note rate plus MIP.

   NOTE: The initial balance at origination, scheduled monthly payments, and servicing fees, if any, are not included in D, and that D is subject to per diem interest and MIP if mid-month calculations are made), and R and T are the fixed set-aside amounts for repairs after closing and first year taxes and insurance as required. NOTE: Once repairs and first year taxes and insurance have been paid, R and T become zero for the remainder of the loan.

6. Scheduled Monthly Payments:

   $P = (\ NPL\{Sub\ k\} - [\ LOC\{Sub\ k\} - D\{Sub\ k\}\ ]\ ) \times (1 + i)\{Sup\ m\} \times i\ /\ [(1 + i)\ \{Sup\ (m-1)\} - (1 + i)]$, where P is the maximum scheduled monthly payment to the borrower commencing in month k and continuing for a term of m months, [For a tenure payment, m is calculated to be: $m = 12 \times (100 - \text{Borrower's Initial Age}) - k + 1$. For any term less than that of a tenure payment, the borrower may choose the number of months, m. For calculation of monthly payment amount at loan origination, set $k = 1$ in all equations. Note that for mid-month originations, the first payment will be made in the second month. For payment plan modifications, principal limits and loan balances will be calculated as of the effective date of the modification, which is the date of first modified payment.]

   $NPL\{Sub\ k\}$ is the net principal limit from equation (3), $LOC\{Sub\ k\}$ is the principal limit of the line of credit from equation (4), and $D\{Sub\ k\}$ is the portion of the loan balance attributable to the line of credit as defined in equation (5). Note that the difference $(LOC\{Sub\ k\} - D\{Sub\ k\})$ may be interpreted as the net principal limit of the line of credit, and $(\ NPL\{Sub\ k\ \} - [LOC\{Sub\ k\} - D\{Sub\ k\}]\ )$ may be interpreted as net principal limit available for calculating monthly payments.

HUD Field Offices

ALABAMA

Birmingham Field Office
950 22nd St North
Suite 900
Birmingham, AL 35203-5302
Phone: (205) 731-2617
Fax: (205) 731-2593

ALASKA

Anchorage Field Office
3000 C. Street
Suite 401
Anchorage, AK 99503
Phone: (907) 677-9800
Fax: (907) 677-9803

ARIZONA

Phoenix Field Office
One N. Central Avenue
Suite 600
Phoenix, AZ 85004
Phone: (602) 379-7100
Fax: (602) 379-3985

Tucson Field Office
160 North Stone Avenue
Tucson, AZ 85701-1467
Phone: (520) 670-6000
Fax: (520) 670-6207

ARKANSAS

Little Rock Field Office
425 West Capitol Avenue
Suite 1000
Little Rock, AR 72201-3488
Phone: (501) 324-5931
Fax: (501) 324-6142

CALIFORNIA

San Francisco Regional Office
600 Harrison St. 3rd Floor
San Francisco, CA 94107-1300
Phone: (415) 489-6400
Fax: (415) 489-6419

Fresno Field Office
855 M Street
Suite 970
Fresno, CA 93721
Phone: (559) 487-5033
Fax: (559) 487-5191

Los Angeles Field Office
611 W. Sixth Street
Suite 800
Los Angeles, CA 90017
Phone: (213) 894-8000
Fax: (213) 894-8110

Sacramento Field Office
John E. Moss Federal
Building
Room 4-200
650 Capitol Mall
Sacramento, CA 95814
Phone: (916) 498-5220
Fax: (916) 498-5262

San Diego Field Office
Symphony Towers
750 B Street
Suite 1600
San Diego, CA 92101-8131
Phone: (619) 557-5310
Fax: (619) 557-5312

Santa Ana Field Office
Santa Ana Federal Building
Room 7015
34 Civic Center Plaza
Santa Ana, CA 92701-4003
Phone: (714) 796-5577
Fax: (714) 796-1285

COLORADO
Denver Regional Office
1670 Broadway, 25th Floor
Denver, CO 80202
Phone: (303) 672-5440
Fax: (303) 672-5004

CONNECTICUT
Hartford Field Office
One Corporate Center
20 Church Street
19th Floor
Hartford, CT 06103-3220
Phone: (860) 240-4800
Fax: (860) 240-4850

DELAWARE
Wilmington Field Office
920 King Street
Suite 404
Wilmington, DE 19801-3016
Phone: (302) 573-6300
Fax: (302) 573-6259

DISTRICT OF COLUMBIA
Washington, DC Field Office
820 First Street NE
Suite 300
Washington, DC 20002-4205
Phone: (202) 275-9200
Fax: (202) 275-9212

FLORIDA
Miami Field Office
909 SE First Avenue
Miami, FL 33131
Phone: (305) 536-5678
Fax: (305) 536-5765

Jacksonville Field Office
Charles E. Bennett Federal Building
400 W. Bay Street, Suite 1015
Jacksonville, FL 32202
Phone: (904) 232-2627
Fax: (904) 232-3759

Orlando Field Office
3751 Maguire Boulevard
Room 270
Orlando, FL 32803-3032
Phone: (407) 648-6441
Fax: (407) 648-6310

Tampa Field Office
500 Zack Street
Suite 402
Tampa, FL 33602
Phone: (813) 228-2026
Fax: (813) 228-2431

GEORGIA
Atlanta Regional Office
40 Marietta Street
Five Points Plaza
Atlanta, GA 30303-2806
Phone: (404) 331-5001
Fax: (404) 730-2392

HAWAII
Honolulu Field Office
500 Ala Moana Blvd.
Suite 3A
Honolulu, HI 96813-4918
Phone: (808) 522-8175
Fax: (808) 522-8194

IDAHO
Boise Field Office
Plaza IV, Suite 220
800 Park Boulevard
Boise, Idaho 83712-7743
Phone: (208) 334-1990
Fax: (208) 334-9648

ILLINOIS
Chicago Regional Office
Ralph Metcalfe Fed Building
77 West Jackson Boulevard
Chicago, IL 60604-3507
Phone: (312) 353-5680
Fax: (312) 886-2729

Springfield Field Office
500 W. Monroe St.,
Suite 1 SW
Springfield, IL 62704
Phone: (217) 492-4120
Fax: (217) 492-4154

INDIANA
Indianapolis Field Office
151 North Delaware Street
Suite 1200
Indianapolis, IN 46204-2526
Phone: (317) 226-6303
Fax: (317) 226-6317

IOWA
Des Moines Field Office
210 Walnut Street
Room 239
Des Moines, IA 50309-2155
Phone: (515) 284-4512
Fax: (515) 284-4743

KANSAS
Kansas City Regional Office
400 State Avenue
Room 507
Kansas City, KS 66101-2406
Phone: (913) 551-5462
Fax: (913) 551-5469

KENTUCKY
Louisville Field Office
601 West Broadway
Louisville, KY 40202
Phone: (502) 582-5251
Fax: (502) 582-6074

LOUISIANA
New Orleans Field Office
Hale Boggs Federal Building
500 Poydras Street, 9th Floor
New Orleans, LA 70130
Phone: (504) 589-7201
Fax: (504) 589-7266

Shreveport Field Office
401 Edwards Street
Room 1510
Shreveport, LA 71101-5513
Phone: (318) 226-7030
Fax: (318) 676-3506

MAINE
Bangor Field Office
202 Harlow Street -
Chase Building
Suite 101
Bangor, ME 04401-4919
Phone: (207) 945-0467
Fax: (207) 945-0533

MARYLAND
Baltimore Field Office
5th Floor
10 South Howard Street
Baltimore, MD 21201-2505
Phone: (410) 962-2520
Fax: (410) 209-6670

MASSACHUSETTS
Boston Regional Office
10 Causeway Street
Room 301
Boston, MA 02222-1092
Phone: (617) 994-8200
Fax: (617) 565-6558

MICHIGAN
Detroit Field Office
477 Michigan Avenue
Detroit, MI 48226-2592
Phone: (313) 226-7900
Fax: (313) 226-5611

Flint Field Office
Phoenix Building
801 South Saginaw, 4th Floor
Flint, Michigan 48502
Phone: (810) 766-5112
Fax: (810) 766-5122

Grand Rapids Field Office
Trade Center Building
50 Louis Street, N.W.
Grand Rapids, MI 49503-2633
Phone: (616) 456-2100
Fax: (616) 456-2114

MINNESOTA
Minneapolis Field Office
Kinnard Financial Center
920 Second Avenue South
Minneapolis, MN 55402
Phone: (612) 370-3000
Fax: (612) 370-3220

MISSISSIPPI
Jackson Field Office
McCoy Federal Building
100 W. Capitol Street
Room 910
Jackson, MS 39269-1096
Phone: (601) 965-4757
Fax: (601) 965-4773

MISSOURI
St. Louis Field Office
1222 Spruce Street
Suite 3207
St. Louis, MO 63103-2836
Phone: (314) 539-6583
Fax: (314) 539-6384

MONTANA
Helena Field Office
7 W 6th Ave
Helena, MT 59601
Phone: (406) 449-5050
Fax: (406) 449-5052

NEBRASKA
Omaha Field Office
Edward Zorinsky Federal Bldg
1616 Capitol Avenue
Suite 329
Omaha, NE 68102-4908
Phone: (402) 492-3101
Fax: (402) 492-3150

NEVADA
Las Vegas Field Office
300 S. Las Vegas Blvd.
Suite 2900
Las Vegas, NV 89101-5833
Phone: (702) 366-2100
Fax: (702) 388-6244

Reno Field Office
745 West Moana Lane
Suite 360
Reno, Nevada 89509-4932
Phone: (775) 824-3703
Fax: (775) 784-5005

NEW HAMPSHIRE
Manchester Field Office
Norris Cotton Federal Bldg
275 Chestnut Street
4th Floor
Manchester, NH 03101
Phone: (603) 666-7510
Fax: (603) 666-7667

NEW JERSEY
Newark Field Office
One Newark Center
13th Floor
Newark, NJ 07102-5260
Phone: (973) 622-7900
Fax: (973) 645-2323

Camden Field Office
Bridgeview Bldg., 2nd floor
800-840 Cooper Street
Camden, NJ 08102-1156
Phone: (856) 757-5081
Fax: (856) 757-5373

NEW MEXICO
Albuquerque Field Office
625 Silver Avenue SW
Suite 100
Albuquerque, NM 87102
Phone: (505) 346-6463
Fax: (505) 346-6704

NEW YORK

New York Regional Office
26 Federal Plaza
Suite 3541
New York, NY 10278-0068
Phone: (212) 264-8000
Fax: (212) 264-3068

Albany Field Office
52 Corporate Circle
Albany, NY 12203-5121
Phone: (518) 464-4200
Fax: (518) 464-4300

Buffalo Field Office
Lafayette Court
2nd Floor
465 Main Street
Buffalo, NY 14203-1780
Phone: (716) 551-5755
Fax: (716) 551-5752

Syracuse Field Office
128 E. Jefferson Street
Syracuse, NY 13202
Phone: (315) 477-0616
Fax: (315) 477-0196

NORTH CAROLINA

Greensboro Field Office
Asheville Building
1500 Pinecroft Road
Suite 401
Greensboro, NC 27407-3838
Phone: (336) 547-4001
Fax: (336) 547-4138

NORTH DAKOTA

Fargo Field Office
657 2nd Avenue North
Room 366
Fargo, ND 58108
Phone: (701) 239-5136
Fax: (701) 239-5249

OHIO

Columbus Field Office
200 North High Street
Columbus, OH
43215-2463
Phone: (614) 469-2540
Fax: (614) 469-2432

Cincinnati Field Office
632 Vine St. Fifth Floor
Cincinnati, OH 45202
Phone: (513) 684-3451
Fax: (513) 684-6224

Cleveland Field Office
1350 Euclid Avenue
Suite 500
Cleveland, OH 44115-1815
Phone: (216) 522-4058
Fax: (216) 522-4067

OKLAHOMA

Oklahoma City Field Office
301 NW 6th Street
Suite 200
Oklahoma City, OK 73102
Phone: (405) 609-8509
Fax: (405) 609-8588

Tulsa Field Office
Williams Center Tower II
2 West Second Street
Suite 400
Tulsa, OK 74103
Phone: (918) 292-8900
Fax: (918) 292-8993

OREGON

Portland Field Office
400 SW 6th Avenue
Suite 700
Portland, OR 97204-1632
Phone: (971) 222-2600
Fax: (971) 222-0357

PENNSYLVANIA

Philadelphia Regional Office
The Wanamaker Building
100 Penn Square, East
Philadelphia, PA
19107-3380
Phone: (215) 656-0500
Fax: (215) 656-3445

Pittsburgh Field Office
339 Sixth Avenue
Sixth Floor
Pittsburgh, PA 15222-2515
Phone: (412) 644-6428
Fax: (412) 644-4240

RHODE ISLAND

Providence Field Office
121 South Main Street
Suite 300
Providence, RI 02903-7104
Phone: (401) 277-8300
Fax: (401) 277-8398

SOUTH CAROLINA

Columbia Field Office
1835 Assembly Street
13th Floor
Columbia, SC 29201-2480
Phone: (803) 765-5592
Fax: (803) 253-3043

SOUTH DAKOTA

Sioux Falls Field Office
4301 West 57th Street
Suite 101
Sioux Falls, SD 57108
Phone: (605) 330-4223
Fax: (605) 330-4428

TENNESSEE

Nashville Field Office
235 Cumberland Bend
Suite 200
Nashville, TN 37228-1803
Phone: (615) 736-5600
Fax: (615) 736-7848

Knoxville Field Office
710 Locust Street, SW
Suite 300
Knoxville, TN 37902-2526
Phone: (865) 545-4370
Fax: (865) 545-4569

Memphis Field Office
200 Jefferson Avenue
Suite 300
Memphis, TN 38103-2389
Phone: (901) 544-3367
Fax: (901) 544-3697

TEXAS
Ft. Worth Regional Office
801 Cherry Street, Unit #45
Suite 2500
Ft. Worth, TX 76102
Phone: (817) 978-5965
Fax: (817) 978-5567

Dallas Field Office
525 Griffin Street
Room 860
Dallas, TX 75202-5032
Phone: (214) 767-8300
Fax: (214) 767-8973

Houston Field Office
1301 Fannin
Suite 2200
Houston, TX 77002
Phone: (713) 718-3199
Fax: (713) 718-3225

Lubbock Field Office
1205 Texas Avenue
Room 511
Lubbock, TX 79401-4093
Phone: (806) 472-7265
Fax: (806) 472-7275

San Antonio Field Office
One Alamo Center
106 South St. Mary's Street,
Suite 405
San Antonio, TX 78205-3625
Phone: (210) 475-6806
Fax: (210) 472-6804

UTAH
Salt Lake City Field Office
125 South State Street
Suite 3001
Salt Lake City, UT 84138
Phone: (801) 524-6070
Fax: (801) 524-3439

VERMONT
Burlington Field Office
159 Bank Street
2nd Floor
Burlington, VT 05401
Phone: (802) 951-6290
Fax: (802) 951-6298

VIRGINIA
Richmond Field Office
600 East Broad Street
Richmond, VA 23219-4920
Phone: (804) 771-2100
Fax: (804) 822-4984

WASHINGTON
Seattle Regional Office
909 First Avenue
Suite 200
Seattle, WA 98104-1000
Phone: (206) 220-5101
Fax: (206) 220-5108

Spokane Field Office
US Courthouse Building
920 W. Riverside, Suite 588
Spokane, WA 99201-1010
Phone: (509) 368-3200
Fax: (509) 368-3209

WEST VIRGINIA
Charleston Field Office
405 Capitol Street
Suite 708
Charleston, WV 25301-1795
Phone: (304) 347-7000
Fax: (304) 347-7050

WISCONSIN
Milwaukee Field Office
310 West Wisconsin Avenue
Room 1380
Milwaukee, WI 53203-2289
Phone: (414) 297-3214
Fax: (414) 297-3947

WYOMING
Casper Field Office
150 East B Street
Room 1010
Casper, WY 82601-1969
Phone: (307) 261-6250
Fax: (307) 261-6245

Glossary

Acceleration Clause: a clause in the contract that states when and under what circumstances a loan may be declared due and payable.

Adjustable Rate: any interest rate that changes based on a market index or is tied to a specific interest rate on a security such as a Treasury bill or Bond.

Annuity: a contract between two parties, under which a predetermined series of payments usually made on a monthly basis for a predetermined period of time are agreed upon.

Appraisal: an estimation of the market value of a specific home in a specific market area at a specific time.

Appreciation: any increase in the market value of the house over a specific period of time.

Arbitrage: a strategy where a person borrows money at one rate in an effort to invest it in something else at a higher rate.

Area Agency on Aging (AAA): a local or regional nonprofit organization that provides information on services and programs for older adults.

Cap: the maximum increase for any adjustable interest rate during a specified time period.

Closing: the final meeting where all parties sign all required documentation to put a mortgage in place. It is also the beginning date of the mortgage.

Condemnation: the legal term used when a court declares a specific property to be unfit or unsafe for public or private use.

Credit Line: a predetermined amount set aside for an individual account from which a borrower may access the funds.

Current Interest Rate: in the HECM program, the interest rate currently being charged on a loan. It equals the one-year rate for U.S. Treasury Securities, plus a margin.

Dead Equity: the equity buildup within a retired person's or couple's primary residence. It is referred to as dead equity because, technically, home equity has a zero rate of return and is not liquid.

Deferred Payment Loans (DPLs): any loan which delays the repayment of principal and interest until some future date or event. Although regular payments are not required, the interest on these loans continues to accrue until such time as the loan is settled in full.

Depreciation: any decrease in the market value of the house over a specific period of time.

Eminent Domain: the law that gives federal, state, county, and municipal governments the right to make a claim on private property for public use.

Expected Interest Rate: the interest rate used to determine a borrower's loan advance amounts. It equals the average rate for U.S. Treasury Securities over the last ten years, plus a margin.

Fannie Mae: a private company that buys and sells mortgages. Although not government-owned, most aspects of its operation are watched over by the federal government.

Federal Housing Administration (FHA): an agency of the U.S. Department of Housing and Urban Development (HUD) that insures HECM loans.

Federally Insured Reverse Mortgage: a reverse mortgage guaranteed by the federal government; also know as a Home Equity Conversion Mortgage (HECM).

Fixed Monthly Loan Advances: payments made to the borrower on a monthly basis.

Home Equity: the difference between a home's market value and any unpaid balance of the mortgage and/or an attached equity line credit or other outstanding debt tied by contract to that home.

Home Equity Conversion: the process in which a homeowner can access equity in the form of cash without having to make regular principal and interest payments or vacate the premises.

Home Equity Conversion Mortgage (HECM): the only reverse mortgage program insured by the Federal Housing Administration.

Home Equity Management: the practice of taking advantage of favorable interest and tax rates by using loans against the equity of a home and investing the money elsewhere.

HUD: Department of Housing and Urban Development.

Initial Draw: if more than one method of receiving the funds is used, the amount that is received at closing (really 3 days after closing) is the Initial Draw. Example: if the Net Amount is $50,000 and the borrower wanted $20,000 in a lump sum at closing and $30,000 left in a Line of Credit, the $20,000 would be the Initial Draw.

Initial Interest Rate: in the HECM program, the interest rate that is first charged on the loan beginning at closing. It equals the one-year rate for U.S. Treasury Securities, plus a margin.

Leftover Equity: the sale price of the home minus the total amount owed on it and the cost of selling it; the amount the homeowner or heirs get when the house is sold.

Lending Limit: the dollar figure set by the FHA. Regardless of the actual value of a home, this is the maximum loan permitted.

Line of Credit: one of the methods of distribution of the cash available in a reverse mortgage. Limited to the total amount at the time the loan is made, a line-of-credit provides the borrower with the options of when to take cash and how much.

Loan Advances: payments made to a borrower, or to another party on behalf of a borrower.

Loan Balance: the amount owed, including principal and interest; capped in a reverse mortgage by the value of the home when the loan is repaid.

Lump Sum: a single loan advance at closing.

Margin: in the HECM program, the amount added to the one-year Treasury rate to determine the initial and current interest rates, and to the 10-year Treasury rate to determine the expected interest rate.

Maturity: when a loan must be repaid; when it becomes due and payable.

Maximum Claim Amount: on the HECM product, this is the lesser of the appraised value or the lending limit. On Jumbo programs, it's the appraised value. The Maximum Claim Amount is the figure that's used to begin the calculations.

MIP: mortgage insurance required by the FHA. It pays if the principal amount is exceeded or if the amount owed on the reverse mortgage at sale would be greater than the sale price.

Mortgage: a legal document making a home available to a lender to repay a debt.

Net Principal Limit: the amount of entitlement (Principal Limit) minus Service Fee Set Aside and minus Total Fees and Costs but before the debt payoff amount is deducted.

Nonrecourse Mortgage: a home loan in which the borrower can never owe more than the home's value at the time the loan is repaid.

Origination: the process of setting up a mortgage, including preparing documents.

Origination Fee: the maximum allowed, up to 2% on a sliding scale, by HUD to go to the lender. This is all the lender can make on the front end of the loan. Stated another way, no processing, application, administration, etc. fee can be charged by the lender.

Other Closing Costs: the terminology differs from lender to lender. Some call Other Closing Costs everything other than the Service Fee Set-Aside. This may include Origination, 2% Mortgage Insurance Premium, and what many call regular closing costs (costs associated with any mortgage – attorney fee, title search, intangible tax, lenders title insurance, etc.). Some lenders itemize the costs differently and Other Closing Costs only refers to what is considered regular closing costs.

Property Tax Deferral (PTD): reverse mortgages that pay annual property taxes; usually offered by state or local governments.

Principal Limit: the amount of the lending limit based on the age of borrower.

Property Appraised Value: the value as determined by a certified appraiser.

Proprietary Reverse Mortgage: a reverse mortgage product owned by a private company.

Reverse Mortgage: also known as lifetime mortgage in the United Kingdom. This is a loan available to seniors (62 and over in the United States) used to release the home equity in the property as one lump sum or multiple payments. The homeowner's obligation to repay the loan is deferred until the owner dies, the home is sold, or the owner leaves.

Reverse Mortgage Annuity: a reverse mortgage in which a lump sum is used to purchase an annuity that gives the borrower a monthly income for life.

Right of Rescission: all reverse mortgages contain a provision that gives a borrower the right to cancel a home loan within three business days of the closing date.

Servicing: administering a loan after closing, such as maintaining loan records and sending statements.

Shared Equity: an itemized loan cost based on a percent of a home's value at loan maturity; for example, a 5% shared equity fee on a home worth $200,000 at maturity would be $10,000.

Supplemental Security Income (SSI): a federal monthly income program for low-income persons who are age 65+, blind, or disabled.

Tenure Advances: fixed monthly loan advances for as long as a borrower lives in a home.

Term Advances: fixed monthly loan advances for a specific period of time.

Total Annual Loan Cost (TALC) rate: the projected annual average cost of a reverse mortgage including all itemized costs.

T-Rate: the rate for U.S. Treasury Securities; used to determine the initial, expected, and current interest rates for the HECM program.

Uninsured reverse mortgage: a reverse mortgage that becomes due and payable on a specific date.

203(b) limit: the dollar limit (formerly, for each county) for how much of a home's value can be used to determine the amount of money a person can get from a federally insured HECM reverse mortgage. The name comes from Section 203(b) of the National Housing Act.